Understanding Ourselves

J Krishnamurti

Books by J. Krishnamurti

The Awakening of Intelligence
Education and the Significance
of Life
The Ending of Time
Exploration into Insight
The First and Last Freedom
A Flame of Learning
The Flame of Attention
The Flight of the Eagle
Freedom from the Known
Freedom, Love and Action
The Future Is Now
The Future of Humanity
The Impossible Question
Krishnamurti's Journal
Krishnamurti's Notebook
Krishnamurti on Education
Krishnamurti to Himself
Letters to the Schools
Life Ahead
This Light in Oneself
The Limits of Thought
Meditations
Meeting Life
The Network of Thought
The Only Revolution

On Conflict
On Fear
On Freedom
On God
On Learning and Knowledge
On Living and Dying
On Love and Loneliness
On Mind and Thought
On Nature and the Environment
On Relationship
On Right Livelihood
On Truth
Penguin Krishnamurti Readers
Questioning Krishnamurti
Reflections on the Self
Talks with American Students
Think on These Things
This Light in Oneself
Total Freedom
Truth and Actuality
Washington DC Talks
A Wholly Different Way of
Living
The Wholeness of Life
Collected Works in 17 volumes
(Talks 1933 to 1967)

Available from:
Krishnamurti Foundation Trust
Brockwood Park, Bramdean, Hants SO24 0LQ, UK

Krishnamurti Foundation of America
P O Box 1560, Ojai CA93024-1560, USA

Krishnamurti Foundation India
Vasanta Vihar, 64/5 Greenways Road, Chennai 600 028, India

Understanding Ourselves

J Krishnamurti

Celebrating the First Thirty Years
of Brockwood Park School

Krishnamurti Foundation Trust, Ltd 1999

Understanding Ourselves

Edited by Ray McCoy

For information about the Krishnamurti Foundation Trust, Brockwood Park School, and the Krishnamurti Centre, please contact:
Krishnamurti Foundation Trust
Brockwood Park
Bramdean, Hants SO24 0LQ, UK
E-mail: kft@brockwood.org.uk

Krishnamurti, J. (1895 – 1986)

ISBN 0-900506-14-8

Contents

Part One
Understanding Ourselves
The First Public Talks and Discussions at Brockwood Park in 1969

Part Two
Shattering all Conditioning
Krishnamurti and Education at Brockwood Park School

Foreword

Krishnamurti gave these public talks to large audiences at Brockwood Park in the first year of the School's existence.

It seems particularly appropriate that they should be published again now, to mark Brockwood's Thirtieth Year Anniversary. This new edition also includes a dialogue between Mary Zimbalist and Mary Cadogan, who are two of the Trustees. Their discussion took place at the Brockwood Park Educational Centre in 1997, and it describes Krishnamurti's approach to starting the School and his deep, continuing involvement in it.

Part One

Understanding Ourselves

LIVING WITHOUT RESISTANCE

I feel that I ought to be sitting on the ground with all the rest of you instead of up here on this platform. I think it must be understood from the very beginning that this is not a position of authority. I'm not sitting up here as a kind of Delphic Oracle laying down the law or trying to persuade you to any particular kind of attitude, action or thought. But since we are here, apparently in all seriousness, and since you have taken the trouble to come, I think we ought to find out why human beings throughout the world live in isolation, divided by their particular beliefs, pleasures, problems and ideals. We find them belonging to various groups such as the Communists, the socialists, the Christians, Hindus and Buddhists, all further dividing themselves into innumerable sects with their own particular dogmas.

Why do we live with this sense of duality, opposing each other at all levels of our existence, resisting each other and bringing about conflict and war? This has been the pattern of human activity throughout the world probably from the very beginning of time—this sense of separation dividing the artist, the soldier, the musician, the scientist, the so-called religious man, the man of business. Although they talk of love and peace on earth, in this way there can be no peace, in this way we must be at war with each other. One wonders whether it must always be like this.

Is it possible for human beings who are serious to find out if they can live in a state of non-duality, not ideologically or theoretically, but actually, both in form and essence? Is it at all possible for you and me to live a life in which this sense of duality ceases completely, not only at the verbal level, but also in the deeper layers and recesses

3

of the mind? I feel that if this is not possible, then we must continue at war with each other, you with your particular opinions, beliefs, dogmas and conclusions and I with mine, so there is never real communication or contact.

Here we are confronted with this issue, not ideologically but actually. One of the major political problems is the unity of mankind. Is it at all possible? Can individuals, you and I, live a life in which there is no duality at all, in which opinions, beliefs and conclusions do not divide people or bring about resistance? If we put that question to ourselves, deeply with all our heart, our whole being, I wonder what our response would be? Can we freely inquire together into this question?

Communication and relationship always go together. If there is no communication, there is no relationship, not only between you and the speaker, but also between yourselves. If we remain merely at the verbal level, the formal level, communication remains very superficial and doesn't go very far. To be related at the non-verbal level requires the ending of this isolating, dual existence, the 'me' and the 'you', the 'we' and the 'they', the Catholic and the Protestant, and so on. To inquire into the question of whether it is possible to live a life in which there is no sense of separation or division, one must be aware of oneself, because as *we* are, so is the world. The world is not separate from us; the community, the collective, is not separate from each one of us. We *are* the community; we *are* the world.

Now, we may *state* that we are the world, but do we really have the feeling that we are utterly part of this whole world? To go into this question, one must inevitably be aware of the whole structure and the nature of oneself, not only inwardly but also outwardly. The word divides, as "the Englishman", "the Frenchman". Opinions and conclusions bring about separation and isolation, as do sectarian beliefs. Outwardly, my sitting up here on the platform divides. Inwardly, inside the skin as it were, there are also various forms of division and separation whose very essence is the 'me', the self, the ego, put together by thought. Can this process, of which one must be aware outwardly as well as inwardly, be understood and dissolved? I think that is probably the major problem in the world rather than the economic problems. Even living in a Welfare State with all its social security, we find people divided, isolated, each going his own particular way, immersed in his own problems. If we are aware both outwardly and inwardly, can this isolating process, this resistance, really be dissolved?

This is very complex, because it is the very nature of thought to divide, to bring about fragmentation as the observer, the experiencer, the watcher, and the thing that is watched, experienced or observed. There is division, the space created between the observer and the observed. That division is brought about by thought. We are not saying this dogmatically; one can observe it, experiment with it and test it. As we said, there can be no communication as long as there is division. And what we consider to be love will also divide if it is the product of thought or hedged about by thought.

When one becomes aware of all this, what is one to do, how is one to act? Thought must be exercised, logically, sanely, healthily and completely, and yet not create division. If there is sensitivity, which is part of love, then thought has no place in it at all, since thought brings fragmentation, separation and division. So how is one to live in a world that is completely divided and which glories in such division and separation? How is one to live so that there is complete harmony, inwardly as well as outwardly?

5

The moment we have a formula, a system, that very system or formula brings about a separation—your system and my system. So the question "how" doesn't enter into this at all. When I ask myself how I am to live with great sensitivity, which is probably the very essence of love, or how I am to do anything without bringing about separation, the "how" implies a method, a system: by doing this you will achieve this harmony, this state of non-duality. But that very word "how" breeds division. That is, there is the *idea* of harmony—a formula, an ideal, which thought has conceived of as being harmonious, living without division—which is to be the final achievement, and there is a separation between that and the actual state I am in, with the "how" as the medium, the way to that ideal. So the "how" immediately breeds division between 'what is' and 'what should be'.

If one completely discards the "how", the method, the system, then there is no ideology at all, no idea of 'what should be'. Then there is only 'what is', and nothing else. The 'what is' is the fact that the way one lives and feels, thinks, acts, loves, is the way of separation and division. That is the actual fact. Can that fact be transformed into something which is non-dualistic? Can I observe the fact that my life is dualistic, separated and isolated, and that however much I may say to my wife, 'I love you', I live in separation? Because the fact is that I am ambitious, greedy, envious, with antagonisms and hatreds boiling in me. Can the mind look at that fact non-dualistically? That is, can I, the watcher, instead of regarding that fact as something separate from me, look at it without the separation? Can I look, can *the mind* look, not as an observer or an entity that wishes to change or transform what it observes, but look at it without the observer?

6

Can the mind observe only the fact and not what thought says about the fact—the opinions, the conclusions, the prejudices, judgements, the like and dislike, the feelings of frustration and despair—just observe without thought reacting to what is observed? I think that is real awareness: to observe with such sensitivity that the whole brain, which is so conditioned, so heavily burdened with its own conclusions, ideas, pleasures and hopes, is completely quiet and yet alive to what it is observing. Am I making myself clear?

One observes what is happening in the world, the constant political and religious divisions, the wars that are going on all the time, not only between individuals but throughout the world. And one wants to live completely at peace, because one realizes that conflict in any form is not creative, that it is not the ground in which goodness can flower. And this world is part of me; I am the world—not verbally, but actually, inwardly. I have made the world and the world has made me. I am part of this society and this society is being put together by me. Is it possible to live our lives, not only in outward form but deeply inwardly, so that no isolating process is taking place at any time? Because only then is it possible to live in peace, not vegetate but be highly alive, thoughtful and sensitive.

In what way is one to act in daily life without this division; to behave, to talk, to use words so as not to create this division between you and me? Surely it is possible only by being totally aware, completely sensitive, not only to what is going on inwardly, but also outwardly, to the manner of my speech, the words, the gestures, the acts. To be so aware demands a great deal of energy. Do we have that energy? A great deal of energy is necessary to be alert, aware, sensitive. To understand this separating, dualistic life of resistance needs great energy both physically and mentally, the energy of great sensitivity. We ask how all this energy is to come about, knowing that we waste energy in useless talk, through indulging in various forms of images, sexual and otherwise, knowing that energy is spent in ambition and competitiveness that is part of this dualistic process of one's life on which society is built.

Can the mind and the brain, can the whole structure, which is the 'me', be aware of all this, not fragmentarily but totally? That is real meditation—if I may introduce that word rather hesitantly—the mind being aware of itself without creating the observer, the outsider who is looking in. That is only possible when there are no ideologies at all and no sense of achievement; that is, when there is no sense of time. Time, as evolution, exists only when there is the sense of 'what is' and 'what should be'. All the effort, the strain and the struggle to achieve 'what should be' is a great waste of energy. Can one just be aware of the fact that—not knowing what it should do with 'what is (however ugly or beautiful it may be), and not being able to under-stand it or go beyond it—thought has projected the idea of how it *should* be, hoping thereby to overcome 'what is'. But to overcome 'what is', one must take time to do it gradually, slowly, day after day.

Obviously that very way of thinking brings about a division, a separation. Just to observe that, to be completely aware of it highly sensitively—not to think what you should do with it or how to overcome it—is all that the mind can do; to be actually aware of this dualistic process going on all the time, watching how it comes into being, being alert, sensitive only to 'what is' and nothing else. If there is hate, anger, ambition, just be aware of it without trying to transform it. As soon as you try to change it, there

8

is the 'me' who is changing it. But if one is able to observe hate or anxiety, or fear without the observer, *just to observe*, then this whole sense of division, of time, effort and achievement completely comes to an end. Then one can live in the world, both inwardly and outwardly, in a non-dualistic state without resistance.

Can we go into this by asking questions?

Questioner: If you want to live peacefully within yourself, and yet you feel that as part of society you are responsible for what is going on in the world today, how can you live peacefully or with any degree of happiness, knowing the heartrending things that are happening?

Krishnamurti: I have to change myself, that is all. I have to totally and completely transform myself. Is that possible? As long as I consider myself an Englishman, or a Hindu, or belong to any particular group or sect, subscribe to any particular belief, conclusion or ideology, I will continue to contribute to this chaos, this madness around me. Can I then drop these conclusions, prejudices, beliefs and dogmas completely, drop them without effort? If I make an effort, I find myself back immediately in the dualistic world. So can I cease completely to be a Hindu, not only in outward form but in essence? Can I, both outwardly and inwardly, end all sense of competitiveness, the hierarchical approach to life, comparing myself with somebody who is cleverer, richer, more brilliant? Can I do this without any sense of overcoming, without effort? Unless this is done, I am part of this chaos. Such a change is not a matter of time; it must happen now, immediately. If I resolve to change gradually, I will again fall into the trap of division.

So is the mind capable of observing the fact that I am competitive, wanting to fulfil, with all the frustrations, fears, anxieties, guilts and despairs? Can I watch it, see it as a total danger? When one sees something very dangerous, one acts immediately. Approaching a precipice, you don't say, 'I'll go slowly, I'll think about it', you sheer away from it. Do we see the danger of separation, not verbally, but actually? You belong to something and I to something else, each with our own beliefs, our isolating pleasures, sorrows and problems. As long as this state of affairs continues, we must live in chaos. Living in this rather mad, sad and despairing world, with only an occasional burst of joy—the beauty of a cloud, a flower—the question is whether there can be total and complete change.

Q: Asking us to be silently aware of 'what is', seems to be asking too much. It is probably more than we can bear for any length of time without trying to escape from it.

K: If I cannot stand something, I must leave it for a while. Perhaps we see the implications of 'what is', and that is too much. So we cannot give complete attention all the time, we need sometimes to be inattentive. Isn't that so? If there is something I cannot bear, I must leave it for a while and take a rest from it; but during the rest, be attentive to your inattention. Say, I am jealous. Let's take that very common thing. I give all my attention to it and see what is involved: hate, fear, possessiveness, domination, isolation, loneliness, the lack of a companion. And I observe it non-dualistically. If I give it my total attention, I will understand it completely and therefore there needs to be no rest from it. Having understood the danger completely, I have sheered away from it. It is only when I do not give my whole attention, but only partial attention, that I get tired of it, and then I say I must have a rest from the nasty business, and so escape from it. Knowing that we escape from it, and that in escape there is inattention, we are suggesting that we be aware of that inattention. Leave your jealousy, but be aware of that inattention while you are escaping. So that the very inattention becomes attention, which sharpens the mind.

6th September 1969

I think one of our major problems is to be sufficiently sensitive, not only to one's own idiosyncrasies, fallacies and troubles, but also to be sensitive to others. Living in this mechanical world of job, success, competition, ambition, social status and prestige makes for insensitivity to the psychological dangers. One is aware, and naturally so, of the danger of physical insecurity—not having enough money, proper health, clothes and shelter, and so on—but we are hardly aware of our inward psychological structure. One feels that one lacks the finesse, sensitivity and intelligence necessary to deal with the inward problems.

Why is it that we are not as aware of the psychological dangers as we are of the physical ones? We are well aware of the outward dangers—a precipice, poison, snakes, wild animals, or the destructive nature of war. Why is it that we are not completely aware inwardly of the psychological dangers such as nationalism, conflict within oneself, accepting ideologies, concepts and formulas, the danger of accepting authority of any kind, the danger of the constant battles between human beings however closely they may be related? If some of us are aware of those dangers, how do we deal with them? Either we escape from them, suppress them, try to forget them, or leave it to time to resolve them. We do all this because we do not know what else to do. Or, if we have read a great deal, we try to apply what others have said. So there is never a direct contact with the problem. We are always trying to overcome these psychological dangers, to suppress them, trying to force ourselves to understand them; there is never direct communion with the issue. And of course there is the whole modern structure of psychology; the psychologists and analysts want to tell us what we are. They ask us to study the animal so that we will understand ourselves better. Obviously, we are the result of the animal, but we have to understand that *ourselves*, not through the animal or through Freud or Jung or any other specialist, but by seeing what we actually are; understanding it, not through some other person's eyes but with our own eyes, with our own hearts, our own minds. When we do that, all sense of following another, all sense of authority, comes to an end. I think that is very important. Then we do something directly, for its own sake, not because somebody else tells us. I think that is the beginning of what it means to love.

So, can we be aware of, or become sensitive to, the psychological dangers we have so carefully cultivated? When we do become aware of them, how are we to deal with them? Are they to be dissolved through analysis, through introspection? Do we understand the dangers of the psychoanalytic process, whether done by a professional or by oneself? Do the dangers disappear, does time dissolve them? Or are they dissolved by escaping, by suppression, transmutation, or by ignoring them through boredom?

Just as a person to be analysed is conditioned, so also is the analyser. Whether he is a professional or not, he is conditioned by his background, by his particular idiosyncrasies, and his knowledge of what Jung or Freud or some other modern expert has to say. If the professional cannot help us to dissolve completely the psychological danger in which we live, then what are we to do? Analysis is not the way, because that involves time. If you analyse yourself very carefully, step by step, your analysis must be so free of any prejudice or bias, so complete that each analysis does not carry over the knowledge of the past.

Otherwise you are using that which is dead to try to understand that which is living. All this involves time, and if one has to analyse everything every day, one has neither the time nor the energy. One might be able to do it towards the end of one's life, but by then life is finished.

One might try to understand oneself through one's dreams. Probably most of us dream a great deal, and it is said that unless we dream we may go mad, that dreaming is a necessary part of existence. But one must question this understanding of oneself through dreams. They, too, need interpretation; and who is to interpret them, the professional, or yourself? Such interpretation must be done very carefully and correctly. Are you capable of that?

If one questions the necessity of dreaming, a totally different avenue may open up. During the day there are strains and stresses, the ugly quarrels, the nagging, the fears, the bullying of others, and so on; there is a constant and conscious everyday struggle. Why should these struggles continue when one goes to sleep? I think sleep may have a totally different meaning. Why cannot the brain, which has been so active throughout the day, protecting itself, thinking and planning, rest completely quiet when it goes to sleep, so that when it wakes up the next morning it is rejuvenated, fresh and unburdened? I do not know if you have experimented with this, not according to the experts, but for yourself. If you have gone into it sufficiently deeply, I am sure you have found that a brain that is so quiet, so relaxed, so extraordinarily alert and orderly, arrives at a different state altogether. I think sleep has great significance in this way. But if sleep is a constant process of thought, of movement and reaction of the brain, then that sleep is a disturbance, and in that there is no rest.

So is it possible not to dream at all, since we know that unless there is order in our daily existence we must dream, as that is a way of receiving intimations from the unconscious? Can the brain be so awake during the day, so free to observe and examine all its own reactions, its conditioning, its fears, motives, anxieties, guilts, neither suppressing nor avoiding anything, so awake that there is order? It is extraordinarily interesting if you go into all this yourself, not letting somebody else do it for you. You see, unless there is order, the brain is disturbed, which means a neurotic state, because a disorderly life is a neurotic state. And the more disorderly it is, the more the dreams and tensions go on. The brain demands order because in order there is security. Any animal constantly shaken and disturbed will feel very insecure, and go mad also.

So the brain demands order, but not order according to a design or blueprint, or what society calls order. What society regards as order is actually disorder. The brain needs order to be completely secure. It must be secure, not in the sense that it must resist, guard or isolate itself; but it is only secure, orderly, when there is tremendous understanding. Otherwise, when you go to sleep there is a great deal of disturbance, with the brain continuing to try to put things in order.

Dreams, analysis, time, do not solve our psychological dangers and problems. Time is postponement; time is involved as the distance between the fact and the idea of 'what should be'. When thought creates time, it brings about disorder. Time is actually a form of laziness; but in the face of physical danger, you don't say, 'I will act later', you act immediately. So time, analysis, dreams, suppression, sublimation, or any form of escape from or conflict with a problem does not solve it.

Then what is one to do? We have said that analysis is not the way. We have understood what is implied in that, not because somebody has said so, but because we have examined it, experimented with it and observed it, and have put it aside. Through negation of what is considered the positive, we can then face the fact. Now, are we prepared to put aside the whole technique of analysis and introspection completely? In that question a great deal is involved, especially as most of us live in the past. We *are* the past. What happened yesterday shapes the present and so tomorrow. Every day we are being reborn in the shadow of yesterday. So, in asking whether the mind can be made fresh, it is essential to view the whole question of analysis with clarity, and find out for ourselves where memory, which is the past, and the action of memory are necessary and also where they are totally unnecessary and dangerous.

Suppose you insulted me yesterday, why should I carry that burden today? Or you may have flattered me, why should I let it influence me today? Why cannot I finish with it immediately while you are insulting or flattering me? That would mean that I would have to be extraordinarily awake and sensitive as you talked, alert to both your insult and your flattery. As most of us live in the past, our whole brain is the result of the past, of time, of conditioning. With this we are continually responding and reacting: there is a God, or there is no God; we belong to this sect or that; we are Communists or socialists, Catholic or non-Catholic, and so on. So the past, modified, yields the present and the future. Without memory, you would not be able to go to your home, you would not know your name or where you belonged. You cannot live in a state of amnesia, so great watchfulness, that is great sensitivity and therefore great intelligence, are necessary to see where memory is essential and where it is dangerous.

The discarding of all the accepted norms and patterns of existence—that you must analyse, that you must follow, that you must obey, be ambitious, greedy, envious, be moral according to the edicts of society (and therefore actually immoral)—can only come about through the understanding of them. If you do not reject them, you are not free; and if you do reject them, that is if you are capable of rejecting them, it cannot be through mere revolt; that would have no meaning. How, then, is the mind to be aware of itself and its dangers? If it is so aware, what will it do? Having put aside analysis, the sense of time, suppression, all that, how will it deal with the thing of which it is aware? I hope I have made the problem clear. What is the state of the mind that has put aside analysis, time, the understanding of memory, the futility of suppression or escape, and the fallacy of ideologies? Hasn't it become extraordinarily sensitive, not only to the outer but also to the inner? Being highly sensitive and intelligent, how is it going to deal with the fact that it is jealous, or angry, or whatever it is? Not through analysis; all that is out! What will it do, how will it act? And the action must be tested; it must show in form as well as in essence, which means the form must change, because the essence is also changing.

So what is the state of the mind that is aware of its own sorrow—let us use that word for the moment—and how will it deal with it? Can there be any sensitivity if there is a space between the thing that is observed and the observer? Am I sensitive to my wife, or to my neighbour, or to the community, if there is an isolating movement within me, a movement of resistance, of opinion? There would be no relationship and therefore no sensitivity. But, having discarded the fairly obvious things, such as analysis and so on, my mind is extraordinarily sensitive, and therefore it is no longer divided in itself as the observer and the observed.

17

When there is no separation between the observer and the observed, then there is no conflict, and therefore there is immediate action. The mind is aware that it is jealous, gossiping, stupid, envious; those are its reactions, responses. Being sensitive, it has immediate and intimate contact with the response, with the reaction, so there is immediate action. Which means there is no jealousy. And the mind is going to test it. Such a mind is a constant movement, a constant watchfulness, and therefore it is capable of immediate action when necessary.

Questioner: Sir, there is a part of the mind that is moving mechanically and which runs along in spite of awareness of what it is doing. I am aware of certain things going on, emotions and reactions, memories of the past, and so on, but they don't get completely resolved. There is still a sense of separation because the mind is mechanical, it is a habit.

Krishnamurti: How is one to be free of a habit, not any particular habit but habit in general? That is, how is one to be free of the habit of smoking, for example, and the whole machinery of habit in which one lives, the routine?

Q: You were speaking of sleep just now and dreaming in sleep. Surely during the daytime we are also dreaming in a way. Below the surface our minds are dreaming all the time. This is the type of habit I mean.

K: Yes, a habit: the habit of daydreaming, of smoking, of thinking according to a certain formula, the habit of pleasure. We all know what habit means. I was born an Indian, I am going to be an Indian and think as an Indian. That tradition is my habit. Can we go into that?

Q: Are not some habits very deeply inherited from our primitive ancestors?

K: Obviously. The habit of violence is inherited from the animal. We have the habit of obeying and so on.

Q: Would you call an instinct a habit?

K: Maybe. The instinct to kill; you see a little insect and you don't like it, so you tread on it. The instinct to own property and say, 'It's mine, I'm going to build a wall round it'. The instinct that says: 'She is my wife and nobody must touch her or look at her'; 'my family'; 'my country'; 'my God'. First of all we must ask whether there are good habits and bad habits, or if there is only habit.

Q: Are there not good hygienic habits? (Laughter.)

Q: Is love a habit?

K: We shall go into that presently. Is habit right or good in itself, whether hygienic, sexual, instinctual or acquired? We cultivate habits. I've learned how to clean my teeth, and do it very carefully for two or three days, then I get into the habit of it and forget it because it has become a routine. We are questioning whether habit has any value at all.

Q: Cleaning and such things perhaps leave us freer?

K: Habit leaves us free to have other habits! Why do we have habits at all? Is it to have more time for other things? That's what that lady said. Will it give you freedom from habit if you have certain habits? This is a serious question, don't laugh it off. I cultivate certain habits in the hope that I shall have more time to do what is necessary. Does it give me freedom?

Q: Habit comes about by conditioning, so therefore you won't be free.

K: That's just it, sir. Therefore we are questioning the whole value of habit. Habit makes the mind dull, insens-

19

itive and sleepy. By doing the same things over and over again, day after day, like the people who repeat certain words or mantras day after day, the mind is made dull and stupid and quiet.

Q: I think that is not the same as cleaning one's teeth. (Laughter.) Why should we be so aware of that?

K: Why should we have a habit about anything? If cleaning my teeth has become a habit, then I am not paying attention and it may do my teeth a great deal of damage. Take one's sexual habit, it is routine. And that we call love! Is love a habit? We cultivate habits because we want to be secure. We stick to the same food and the same neighbours because we are sure of them. I am sure of my husband, my wife, my children. They are habits. So I see to it that I am surrounded by complete security.

Habit is an avoidance of any questioning, of any further investigation, exploration, of putting things to the test. Can the mind be awake and not form habits? Do please investigate, find out, and be awake when you are cleaning your teeth and therefore highly hygienic. (Laughter.) See that the mind doesn't go to sleep or get dull through habit.

Q: Playing a cello, the more a musician has learnt to play by habit, the less he has to concentrate on the mechanical aspect. He can develop artistic expression.

K: We were talking about this to a musician the other day. He said that to fall into a habit is the very last thing to do; one is learning all the time and therefore habit has no place.

Q: I think there is a different intelligence. We cannot call the playing of an instrument a habit. It is like driving a car; after a time the automatic nervous system deals automatically with the threat of possible danger. A form of intelligence is operating.

K: That's just it. So don't let us talk about good habits and bad habits at all, but question whether the mind, which has been so conditioned in habits, can uncondition itself from all habit—habit being tradition, having an opinion and sticking to it, insisting it is right, believing or not believing in God, calling oneself a Catholic, or a Hindu, or a Buddhist. Have an opinion, but if it's wrong, change it immediately. But why should one have opinions about anything?

Q: But, sir, you have feelings and you express opinions based upon experience in your life.

K: I don't think I'm expressing opinions, I am just stating facts. It is not an opinion to call this a microphone.

Q: You can call it something else.

K: No, I am not calling it something else. I am jealous— full stop. It is not an opinion, it is a fact. I am angry; it is not a conclusion, it is so. I am angry, I am violent, but when I begin to explain what violence is and what you must do about it, say that it should be tackled in this way or that, all that is opinion and conclusion. In facing the fact that one is violent, there is no explaining and no need for opinion. I am brown; there it is; but to say that I shouldn't be brown or that I wish I were a little lighter because that might be more popular, and so on, is silly.

Can we now pursue this to the very end? Can the mind be aware of the habit, whatever it is, and end it instantly, not taking months or years over it? That is only possible when your whole being is aware of that fact, not just a part of your being; not just superficial conscious awareness but being aware of a particular habit, say smoking, with the totality of your being. It means being totally aware of everything that is involved in that habit: the occupation of your hands, your resistance, your pleasure, the poisoning of the body by drugs, and the body demanding more of it, and so on. You see people who are constantly frowning or doing something or other with their hands or face. The immediate perception is the immediate action and the ending of it. But if you say, 'Well, I will take time', you are already finished. The sharpness, the intelligence, the sensitivity of the mind is in the action and the testing of that action.

Q: What do you mean by the testing of that action?

K: Find out, test it. If I smoke, I want to find out all about it, go into it completely. And if I know at the end of it whether to drop it or not to drop it, I have tested it. So habit in any form makes the mind dull, whether it is the habit of pleasure, or the habit of avoiding pain. That means to be on one's toes all the time, watching. It means to learn. Learning is not habit, it is a constant process. Habit forms when you have *accumulated* through learning, which is knowledge. You say, 'I have knowledge, I know'. It is only the stupid man who says, 'I know'. If there is constant learning, how can there be habit, how could habit exist at all?

7th September 1969

KNOWING WHAT LOVE IS

I think most of us are seeking some kind of deep significance or meaning to life. We see what is happening around us, the utter futility of war, the lack of meaning of one's own life, all the divisions—race against race, people against people, one religion against another, the sheer futility and meaninglessness of this whole struggle, only to end up in the grave. So we are seeking some kind of meaning to life. Not finding any, we either worship the state, whether it be the communist or the capitalist state, and we accept a tradition, which either says there is, or there is not, a meaning to life. Or we do not believe in anything and live as entirely in the present as is profitable, convenient and satisfactory.

If one rejects the intellectual patterns invented by the specialists, or by oneself, as well as the mere living of a despairing, meaningless life entirely in the present, one is then faced with a much deeper question; which is, what is this striving about? Education, the family, the acquisition of knowledge and experience, where does it all lead? Will we find the answer to that question in outward relationships, outward activities, objectives and ideologies, or will we find the answer inwardly? And is the inward answer any different from the outward answer? Are the inward and the outward answers mutually dependent, or can we, while living in the outward world and doing the everyday things of life, go so deeply inwardly that we understand? Not intellectually or emotionally or sentimentally, but go so deeply inwardly that the outwardness and the inwardness coalesce, leaving no real outer or inner but only a movement that has its own meaning, a meaning not invented by the mind or by clever, cunning and deceptive thought. Perhaps that may be the answer to the question of whether life has any meaning at all.

To go very deeply inwardly without rejecting the outer—the outer being the form, the action, the responsibilities, the everyday living—to go inwardly in such depth requires tremendous honesty. Not the honesty of conforming to a principle, or an idea, or to some form of pattern that one has set for oneself, that is not honesty at all. Thought can very easily deceive itself and create an illusion and think that it is honest. Surely honesty is to see exactly 'what is' without any distortion, not only outwardly but also inwardly; to see exactly what one is, both at the conscious levels as well as at the deeper levels. To see, if one tells a lie, that it is a lie, just that, without deception, without excuse, without covering it up or escaping from it. When there is such great clarity, when there is that quality of perception, then there is innocency. And only then, I feel, can one begin to understand what love is.

That word "love" is so weighted, so mischievous, ugly and rather destructive. I would like, if I may, to talk a little more about it. The politician uses that word, the housewife uses it, the priest, and also the young girl in love with a boy. So if we talk about it, which is naturally rather difficult, we must, I think, be not only verbally very clear, but also understand the non-verbal process behind it, the very structure of it. That is, there must be an extraordinary sense of clarity and honesty within oneself, which inevitably brings about a quality of innocency. And then, perhaps, we can freely, and yet with great hesitancy, inquire into this word.

First of all, love, surely, is not a sentiment, an emotional state, because sentiment and emotion change, and where there is sentiment and emotion there is a great deal of cruelty. One can get excited about the flag, about one's country, and be ready to kill others. That is a ruthless destructiveness based on sentiment. It can be readily observed in daily life both outwardly and inwardly that where there is any emotional upheaval or surge of sentimentality, it does bring with it a sense of hardness, brutality and violence. Can sentimental and emotional states bring about qualities of gentleness and tenderness or, when there is tenderness, the quality of beauty that goes with being very gentle? Are there not in these states the seeds of ruthlessness and brutality? You can cry over an animal and yet kill it. We can repeat that we are all brothers, that the world is my neighbour, and yet be ready to kill that neighbour—be it in the business world or on the battlefield. That is all brought about through sentimentality and the extravagance of emotionalism. And in all that, obviously, there is no love.

What then is love? Remembering that the word, the description is not the thing, we can see that it is a non-verbal state, and yet it is not pleasure brought about through desire. When pleasure is involved in love, there must also be pain in it, fear, jealousy, the aggressive possessiveness of 'my family', 'my wife', 'my husband', and all the rest of it. Wherever there is the pursuit of pleasure, there must be this sense of domination, possessiveness and attachment, all of which breed a great deal of fear and therefore pain. We have said that love goes with sex. For most of us, love *is* sex. May we go into it a little more, or are you all too grown up, or have finished with it? (Laughter.)

This question of what love is, is really very important. I think one must find out about it for oneself, as one must also find out what living is and what death is. These are the most fundamental questions: what is living; what is love; what is death. They are not to be answered by someone else telling you what they are, for in that there is no freedom. That would be merely copying, imitating, following, depending on your pleasure and your fear. But these questions must be answered. And the more intelligent, the more deeply aware and suffering any human being is, the more deeply must he or she ask them. We have said love is sex; we have put those two words and the activity of those two words together, which means seeing sex as the ultimate pleasure.

What part does thought play in all this? What is the relationship between thought and pleasure? If I am not capable of establishing that relationship clearly, there will always be a quarrel between the two, a division. So I must find out what pleasure is, or rather, if there can be pleasure without thought or whether pleasure is the process of thought. Pleasure to us is extraordinarily important and all our morality is based on that—at any rate social morality, which obviously is not morality at all. Most human beings are pursuing pleasure because they are so discontented, so unhappy, so miserable, so tortured by their environment, by their own thoughts, their own feelings and problems. Freedom, for most human beings, means pleasure and the expression of that pleasure. How does pleasure relate to thought? How does thought give it shape and vitality? One has a certain pleasure, whether it is sexual, or the great pleasure, great enjoyment of seeing a lovely sunset, the beauty of a great tree in the wind, or still water. Then what takes place? Thought steps in and demands, 'I must have it again tomorrow', 'I must see it again the next minute', 'I must enjoy it again as I did that first moment'. So thought comes in and gives it a continuity. This is fairly obvious, if one watches it in oneself. There is sexual activity, followed by imagination and the cultivation of excitement by thought. So thought, by thinking about the sexual pleasure of yesterday, gives it continuity and vitality.

This is the whole process that we call love, and out of that come jealousy, possessiveness and domination. Such love becomes extraordinarily brutal and violent: the love of one's country, the love of God, the love of an ideology for which one is willing to kill another and destroy oneself.

And as thought also creates fear and pain, then where in all this is love? Can one put it into words at all? The words "I love you" are merely a means of communication, and we well know that the word is never the thing, neither linguistically nor semantically. Then what is love? We said that it is obviously not pleasure, that no pleasure is involved in it. It is not desire, not the product of thought. It cannot be cultivated as you would cultivate a rose or a particular quality. It requires a great deal of honesty to find out for oneself what love is, to come upon its beauty and its innocency. Without it life has really no meaning at all. Knowing what love is, we will find most of our questions answered—politically, economically and, if one can use that word, spiritually. So when there is this love, then perhaps we can begin to inquire freely into the whole question of meditation. Because without love meditation becomes utterly infantile.

So honesty, innocency, and this thing called love must be the foundation for meditation. Otherwise it becomes an escape, a cheap affair, a form of self-hypnosis, as with people who pay the money that is always involved in that sort of thing and go through some peculiar initiation and then repeat certain phrases, the very sound of which, they think, will produce a certain result. Surely that is not meditation. To meditate, one needs tremendous intelligence and sensitivity, the intelligence that comes of self-knowledge, the understanding of oneself that comes through knowing oneself completely. To look at oneself with great clarity and honesty is essential, so that there is no possibility of deception. When a mind is so completely honest, it is really innocent. This knowing of oneself brings that sensitivity which is great intelligence and which cannot be bought in any university or acquired through books. You don't have to read a single book about philosophy or psychology, it is all there in yourself. And only when there is this clarity in the knowing and the understanding of oneself, both at the conscious level as well as in the deeper, hidden levels— which is part of meditation—can the mind, uncluttered and free, proceed into things that can never be put into words, that can never be communicated to another.

Please ask questions if you feel it will be of any value, if what has been said has any value.

Questioner: Why is one not orderly on the instant? Is it because of the lack of response?

Krishnamurti: What does that word "orderly" mean? To keep order, as one has order in one's room? Is order brought about through conformity, by imitation of what one considers orderliness to be? I want order within myself because I am disorderly. I am in conflict, I am in contradiction because I find myself driven one day by this desire and the next day by that. I am in a constant state of conflict and contradiction, with burning discontent. And out of this chaos, out of this confusion and disorder, I want order, because I see that if I don't have order I cannot think clearly, I cannot observe, I cannot perceive without distortion.

Order, in the sense we are talking about, has nothing to do with conforming to a particular ideology, or the order of the politician who doesn't want any contradiction, or the order of a religious group which claims to be the sole guardian of the way to truth. We are talking of the order that comes about through understanding the disorder in oneself—the duality, the contradiction and the opposition. Through understanding what disorder is, naturally there comes order. Through the negation of what is disorder comes the positive, which is order, not through conforming to the positive, or what one considers to be order.

Q: Isn't it the trouble of many people that they think about themselves all the time and not about other people?

K: The lady suggests that the real trouble is caused by thinking about oneself instead of about others; that is, my thinking should be rather about you than about myself. You are myself; you are as disorderly, as mischievous, as ugly, as brutal as I am, and if I think about you, my thinking is in actuality also about myself. But let us return to this question of order, because it is really extraordinarily important to understand it.

When you look at our social morality and examine it very closely, you will find that it is completely immoral, completely disorderly. Society allows you to be greedy and envious. That you must seek power, position, prestige, that you will have to fight your way, be violent and competitive, is all considered perfectly respectable, orderly and moral. When you see that, not theoretically but actually, and when you deny all that, then there is order, which is virtue.

The questioner was asking whether that order can be brought about instantly. If one has looked at oneself at all clearly, one can see the disorder, the mischief, the cruelty, the fears and the pleasures in oneself. Can order be born out of that disorder instantly, or must one have time? Time being the gradual bringing about of order within oneself, which may take many days, years or the rest of one's life. Time means eventually. By the time we have explored and freely examined ourselves, gradually cultivating order out of disorder, we shall probably be dead. So one asks whether it is possible to bring about order out of this disorder immediately. Do you not act immediately the instant you see some danger? You don't take time, you don't say, 'I'll think about it'. Where there is the perception of danger, both psychologically and physically, especially when there is bodily danger, there is immediate action. Perception then *is* action, the seeing is the doing, there is no time interval between the seeing and the doing. So why do we not see the real danger; not have an ideological or mere intellectual perception of the danger, but actually see the whole danger of disorder instantly, with the response of our whole being? If you saw it instantly, there would be instant action. If I see a precipice, a snake, or a bus coming, I act instantly because I see the danger of it. It makes an enormous impression on me and I act without any hesitation. What prevents me from looking at myself, in which there is so much disorder, and seeing the danger of it? After all, disorder leads to various neurotic conditions, and I see how dangerous it is not to have order. Order, which is essentially virtue, is a living thing, and where there is order there is greater security. It is only the disorderly person with his disorderly activity, that creates mischief and insecurity.

I do not know if you have observed for yourself how the brain demands order, not habit or routine, but order, a living thing. Have you noticed that most of our day is spent in disorder? Quarrels, aggressiveness, fears, pleasures and competitiveness—that is our day. And as you go to sleep, the brain sets about to bring order within itself, because it cannot live in disorder. If it does, it becomes more and more distorted, and there is the danger of greater insecurity for itself.

So order is essential. The animal demands order, but we have accepted disorder as a way of life. Now what is it that prevents one from seeing the danger and the mischief? The disorder outwardly—the divisions of nationalities with their sovereign governments and armies, the everlasting fragmentation of human beings in their relationships—all that is a tremendous danger. Why don't we see it instantly and drop this nonsensical, meaningless division of "the Englishman", "the Frenchman", and so on? And why do we not see equally clearly the inward danger and mischief that disorder brings about? Is it that we have got used to it, or that we don't know what to do about the disorder? How can a disordered brain do something about its own disorder? If you have the leisure and the money, you go to an analyst. He is also disorderly and has had to undergo analysis himself in order to analyse another. So you are at the mercy of another's disorder.

Is it possible to observe the disorder within oneself instantly, see the danger of it immediately, and end it? I cannot answer for you, obviously, but to end it instantly you must see the total disorder of the inward self, rather than collect the fragmentary disorders and then say, 'I am disorderly'. Surely it is possible to see the totality of disorder in oneself instantly. Otherwise we will continue in this state of confusion, mischief and misery. Is it possible to see your wife or your husband or your neighbour without prejudice and without opinion, to observe without like or dislike? That requires great awareness of oneself. But, you see, one hasn't the time or the energy or the urge. One plays around. And so one accepts wars, disorders, and the confusion and the mischief.

Q: It appears to me that we have to give the time and induce the energy and urge in ourselves in order to go forward in the direction you have indicated.

K: But how will you get that energy, sir? Why do you not have it?

Q: I have other interests.

K: Other interests? When the house is burning? Do the other interests not also create disorder? I may have tremendous interest and energy for some fragment of my life, business or whatever it is. I give thirty or forty years of my life to that interest, while the rest of it is chaos and misery, you know, all the ugliness of it. And that interest concentrated in one fragment is obviously bringing about disorder in other fragments. I am very kind, gentle and affectionate with my family, but in the business world I become a tiger. And then I say to myself, 'I have not the energy to tame that tiger', which is creating so much mischief in my life.

From this arises the question: why do we break up our lives into these compartments—the business world, the family world, the world of golf, the world of God and so on? Why this fragmentation? On one side are the pleasure, the pain, the sorrow, the competitiveness, the aggression, the violence, and on the other the demand for peace. Is it habit, custom, tradition and education, blaming society by thinking, 'If I could only be free of the environment, I would be perfect'? The environment is created by *us*, by our greed, ambitions and brutality. The environment is us.

Until we become aware of ourselves as we are, and change radically—which is the *real* revolution—there can be no possibility of living together in peace. And to do that one must have tremendous energy, not for this or that fragment, but totally.

Q: Does this order, which the brain demands for its security, come about through awareness of oneself, through knowing oneself?

K: Obviously, but not through knowing oneself according to some expert, or some philosopher, or through the speaker, but through looking at oneself, understanding oneself as one is. And to look at oneself is not possible in isolation, or by going into a monastery. Only in relationship can you see all your angers, your jealousies, your domineering, your greed, your assertions and all the rest of it. When one is really aware of oneself—through a gesture or a word, through the manner in which one asserts—the clarity of perception is the instant action of understanding.

Q: Why does awareness of unity come so often to people who know very little and have not studied at all?

K: The questioner asks why primitive people who are not very clever or intellectual, who have not studied or been highly educated, so frequently have this sense of unity, of friendship and generosity. Is it difficult to answer that question? Those people who are educated and highly sophisticated are spoilt; they are the really savage people. They are concerned with their problems, with their own lives, and never look at another, never look at the beauty of the sky, the leaf or the waters. They may see beauty in art galleries or in the pictures they own, but not around them. They are insensitive and are full of knowledge of what other people have said or written.

Q: What is simplicity? And how does this big estate (i.e. Brockwood) fit into it?

K: This estate has thirty-six acres only, the rest is farmland belonging to someone else. This place is a school, which will eventually have about forty to fifty students living here, and for that you must have a large house and the necessary grounds in which to live and play.

And you ask if that is simple. Simplicity is reckoned to be one loin cloth, or one pair of trousers and a coat. Or one meal a day. They have tried this in India, where people talk about a simple life. Monks have tried it, but their lives are not simple at all. Outwardly they may have only one coat and one pair of trousers and eat one meal a day, but the exhibition of outward simplicity is not necessarily inward simplicity. That is something quite different. Simplicity means to have no conflict, no burning desires and no ambitions. You see, we always want the outward show of simplicity, while inwardly we are boiling, burning and destroying. And you ask, 'Why do you have that big house?'—or so many coats, or whatever it is.

As we said, simplicity implies honesty, so that there is no contradiction in oneself. And when there is such a state of mind, there is real simplicity.

13th September 1969

LEARNING IN FREEDOM

I think we might talk about, or rather explore freely into, the question of meditation, which is really a very important question. Before we go into that I feel we should clearly understand the relationship between the speaker and the audience. Here we are investigating, exploring freely, and there is no authority whatsoever, neither of achievement, reputation nor experience. The man who says he knows really does not know, and to explore into this question, which is very serious, demands a great deal of thought, inquiry and freedom. One needs, above all else, freedom from authority; not from the authority of the policeman or the law, but freedom from the authority one brings about because one is so disturbed and uncertain in oneself. In this enormous disorder and confusion we want somebody to tell us how to live, how to meditate and what to think. Thereby we destroy any kind of freedom we may have. If you are going to inquire into this question, there must be freedom from the whole sense of authority, from the authority of the speaker, the authority of books, of tradition, and of what others say they have achieved. Because all of them may be wrong, and probably are wrong. Putting one's faith in another is detrimental to freedom. One must remain free to inquire about everything, not only in politics, which is comparatively easy, but also in the much more difficult area of looking inward and searching. If that is taken for granted, then every intelligent person, whether young or old, will no longer accept any belief or authority about these matters. One has to find out for oneself.

This doesn't mean that you reject what others say, but that you inquire without acceptance or denial. An aggressive mind, a mind tethered to a belief, is not free, and therefore it is incapable of inquiry. All this demands intensive inquiry, not acceptance. The beauty of meditation lies in this very freedom to inquire, not only into outward things but also inwardly, inside the skin, psychologically. So we begin by not accepting any authority.

Perhaps you know the word "guru", which has crept into the English language and which practically everybody uses now. It is a Sanskrit word meaning the one who points, the one who sheds light, the one who alleviates or lightens the burden. There are innumerable gurus all over the world—brown, black, white or pink—who practise various systems of meditation. They say, 'Do these things and you will achieve the most extraordinary states and attain peace'. Since most of us are disturbed both outwardly and inwardly, with minds that are everlastingly chattering to ourselves and burdened with innumerable problems, guilt, anxiety, fear, despair and sorrow, such peace seems highly desirable. One feels that if one could have a few days or a few minutes of absolute quiet, that extraordinary "peace that passes all understanding", one would be able to arrange one's life in an orderly manner. Hence the ready acceptance of systems and methods without a full realization of what is implied in them.

A system implies not only the authority of the one who has achieved and who says, 'I know', but it also means to practise day after day in the hope of achieving some particular result offered by the system, and this must lead to both the system and the one who practises it becoming mechanical. If I practise something daily, over and over again, my mind becomes more and more dulled as it gets caught in the habit of a routine. So one has to reject all systems because they are unintelligent; they make the mind mechanical and they introduce the whole problem of time, promising peace eventually but not now. Somebody comes from Asia offering initiations and enlightenment in return for a certain sum of money, and we are so greedy and thoughtless that we are prepared to accept the method in the hope that we shall come upon that which we think is peaceful. And we reassure ourselves by saying that the system helps. Is that so? Or is it a waste of time altogether?

Take those systems which involve repeating words, especially Sanskrit words, which produce a certain sound which quietens the mind and therefore makes it more observant, not only of outward things but also inwardly. This repeating of a sound, whether it is Ave Maria or some other words, does induce a momentary quietness. But a mind that is dull, unintelligent, insensitive and causing a disorderly life, can repeat any number of words and have some experience of what it calls peace, but it is still a dull mind, incapable of observing deeply all the process of itself. So can we observe this fact—it is not a question of my opinion against your opinion, or your experience against my experience—that a dull mind, which is not capable of looking at things directly but only in a devious manner, frightened, anxious, burdened with innumerable problems, cannot basically be peaceful, though it may repeat thousands of words for a thousand years. Can we, looking at that fact without forming an opinion and seeing the truth of it, put aside all systems? These systems cultivate habit, and a mind caught in habit is not free to observe. Can we completely drop the idea of following someone who offers systems, who gives promises and hopes? It seems to me that is absolutely necessary for a mind to be capable of meditation.

Besides meditation, another major issue is the question of how to bring about order, to live a life of righteousness, which is highly intelligent and sensitive, not intellectual or verbal, but a life in which there is no conflict. For a mind that is in conflict is not a free mind and is incapable of looking at itself, incapable of seeing 'what is'. So our next point is: can the mind bring about order within itself? Because without laying the right foundation, one cannot build anything, and if one is to meditate it is part of that meditation to lay the foundation. This foundation is freedom from opinion. Most of us, as you know, have a thousand opinions about everything. Can the mind be free altogether from opinions, remaining only with 'what is' and nothing else? If the mind can remain with 'what is', it is free of the process of duality. Where there is duality, there is contradiction and therefore conflict.

Please, we are observing ourselves, you are not merely listening to the speaker. In the very act of listening, in seeing the truth or the falseness of what is being said, you are using the speaker, as it were, as a mirror in which you are looking at yourselves. Therefore you are discovering that there can be no perception without distortion as long as there is conflict of any kind in relationship. What is the good of your meditating or seeking God, or whatever it is you seek, if you are jealous of another? It is only when there is freedom from jealousy, from anxiety and guilt, that the mind, being free, can look, learn and act.

So there must be no system and therefore no authority, no following of another. Then ending of all conflict within oneself will bring about a life of righteous behaviour. All this is part of meditation also, to see one's mistakes and to correct them immediately, because perception is action, the seeing is the doing. Then the mind is not carrying over the insults, the flatteries, the anxieties, the hurts; it is free from moment to moment, all the time. It is only in relationship with others that one can begin to discover oneself and see what one actually is; and the understanding of it is the ending of all conflict. A mind that is in conflict is obviously a distorted mind, and however much it may practise meditation, such a mind will only see its own distortion and not something totally new.

Then there is the question of how to observe, how to look, not only outwardly but inwardly. The outer and the inner are one process, it is not a dual process. One can only observe when there is no image through which one is looking. If I have an image about you, I am not looking at *you*, I am looking through the image, or the image is looking at you. That is fairly simple, isn't it? To observe means to have freedom from prejudice, from belief, freedom from any form of distortion. And there is distortion when the mind is tethered to a belief. When the mind is frightened, ambitious, striving to achieve a position of power, and so on, how can it possibly be free to look? So it is very important, it seems to me, to find out what it means to observe, to see; that is, what it means to be aware, to be attentive. Attention is not concentration. Concentration implies the effort to exclude all thought outside one particular issue. We think it is part of meditation to learn to concentrate either on an image or an idea, or to practise certain systems which involve concentration. But where there is concentration there is exclusion and resistance, and where there is resistance there is conflict and the way of duality. I think that is fairly clear?

On the other hand, attention is not exclusion, but just to be aware. This awareness is distorted when observation is coloured by prejudice from which springs a conclusion, when you are conditioned as a believer in some particular form of religious dogma or tradition such as the Christian,

39

Hindu or Buddhist tradition. A conditioned mind is incapable of observation, for it will act, think and experience according to its conditioning. A devout Catholic practising his belief day after day will experience the figure of Christ in his vision or dreams. That only strengthens his conditioning. Such a person is not free to observe; he remains a little bourgeois, caught in his own particular belief, his own particular dogma, inviting the world to enter his cage.

So an essential part of meditation is understanding the difference between concentration and attention. Concentration demands effort,; awareness or attention does not. When one understands this whole process of accepting dogma, tradition, belief, of living in the past, attention comes naturally, and therefore it is a state of mind in which there is no effort. When the mind is completely attentive, you give your whole body, mind and heart, everything you have, to observe and to listen.

And this requires energy. I don't know if you have noticed that when you listen to somebody very carefully, without prejudice, without the interference of your likes and dislikes, then you are attentive. When you are really listening to somebody, there is no 'me' or 'you', there is only the act of listening. That requires energy. If you are listening very attentively now to what is being said, and therefore learning, you are not concentrating, you are completely attentive; therefore there is no division between the speaker and the one who listens—and in this there is involved a great deal more.

Speaking psychologically, is the observer at all different from the thing he observes? When I look at myself, is the observer different from the thing he looks at? If he is different, then there is a division between the thing observed, between that which is experienced, and the experiencer, the observer. It is this difference that brings about conflict and therefore distortion. So one must be very clear and find out directly for oneself whether the observer is the observed, or not. This again is part of what is called meditation. When you go into it very deeply, you will see that the observer *is* the observed. When you are jealous, the jealousy is not different from the entity that observes or is aware of the jealousy. He *is* jealousy. He is the reaction which is called jealousy. When there is no resistance to that thing which he has called "jealousy", but mere observation of the fact, then you will see that the word is not the thing. Jealousy is awakened through the word, through memory, and thereby brings about the observer as different from the observed. The understanding of all that frees the mind from jealousy without effort.

All this is part of meditation, and I hope you are doing it as we are talking. If you don't do it now, you will never do it; it isn't a thing you go home to think about. It is the beauty of meditation that one does it all the time as one is living, every minute of the day as one walks, as one talks, so that the mind becomes acutely aware of itself and therefore highly sensitive, intelligent and deeply honest. Then there is no distortion, no illusion.

It is also part of meditation to find out for oneself, freely, what the nature of thinking is, where the beginning of thought lies, and whether the mind can be completely still to find out when the action of thought is necessary and when it is not; thought being the reaction of knowledge, memory and experience, which is the past. When we are thinking, we are living in the past, we are the past. Though thought may project the future or assert that only the present matters, it is still thought in operation, and thought is the past. For most of us, thought is enormously important

41

because we are living in the past, because we are the past and because all our activities stem from the past. It is part of meditation to find out where the act of thinking is absolutely necessary, logical, healthy and clear, without the interference of any personal like or dislike, and also when thought must be absolutely quiet.

If you have not done all this, meditation has very little meaning. One can meditate in the bus, washing dishes, wiping the floor or talking to another. But perhaps it may help sometimes to sit quietly by yourself, or when you walk by yourself in the woods or in the street, to observe yourself by your reactions, or to be completely quiet. The whole idea of sitting in a certain posture, as they advocate in the East, is very simple. It is to sit straight so that the blood flows to the head properly, whereas if one sits doubled-over, the free passage of the blood is restricted. But if the brain is rather petty, narrow and limited, no amount of blood will prevent it from remaining petty, narrow and stupid. If one is really serious about meditation, one should not only observe what has been said this morning but also see if the body can remain completely quiet.

It is part of meditation to learn all this in oneself. To communicate, one must use words, but there is also a communication which is non-verbal. The non-verbal state of understanding between you and the speaker requires that you also have been through all this, otherwise we cannot possibly communicate. It is like leading someone to the door—the rest of the process you will have to do yourself.

The whole promise of meditation is that you will eventually have a still mind, a mind that is highly awake and able to go into itself to depths impossible for a mind that is full of effort. That is what is generally promised in all these systems. But when one has discarded all the systems one can see the importance of having a quiet mind, not a dull or mechanical mind, but one that is very quiet, very still, observing. Silence, also, is necessary to observe, to listen. If I am continually talking to myself, offering opinions, making judgements and evaluations, have aggressive attitudes because I have certain beliefs, then I am not listening. I can only listen to you when the mind is completely quiet, not resisting, neither agreeing nor disagreeing, but actually listening with my whole being. For that there must be silence. If you would see the beauty of a cloud or a tree, you must look at it with complete quiet. But if, in that quietness, there is the observer who is different from the thing observed, then there is no quiet.

They tell you to take drugs to induce the mind to observe so intensely, so intimately and so fantastically that the space between the observer and the thing observed disappears, or to give you an insight into yourself. Obviously a frightened mind, freed for the moment from fear by taking some drug, might temporarily be enabled to look and listen with that intensity in which there is no observer. But after it has taken that "trip", the fear would still be there, so one would depend inwardly more and more on a drug, a master, a guru, a belief, and so there would be more dependence and more resistance and more fear.

So meditation is the beginning of understanding oneself directly, not through the medium of some drug or drink or excitement, but understanding directly and simply. To understand oneself, to know oneself. The ending of sorrow is the beginning of self-knowing. Most of us are burdened with a great many sorrows, and in the ending of that sorrow lies the understanding of oneself. To understand oneself, one must observe without any distortion, without any like or dislike, without saying, 'This is good, I'll keep it', or,

'This is bad, I'll put it away'. One must observe so that the mind becomes completely alert, both at the conscious level and in the deeper and hidden parts of the mind.

All this, of course, involves much more, but I don't know if we have the time to go into it. There is the question of the nature of the brain, whether the brain, which is so conditioned after thousands of years, can be really quiet, responding only when it is absolutely necessary. That also is part of meditation.

So, when one has gone through all this and understood it, there comes a quietness, a silence that is beyond all verbalization, and which is necessary for the mind if it would understand something beyond itself, beyond the projection of thought and time and bondage, something which man has everlastingly sought—the immortal and the timeless. It is only then, perhaps, that a quiet mind can come upon it.

Do you want to ask any questions about this or about anything else?

Questioner: You spoke just now of a mirror. Is there perhaps an analogy between the mind, inasmuch as we know it, and a photographic camera, in that the camera is a mirror with a memory? The mind, as we know it, is also a mirror with a memory. Should it perhaps be a mirror without a memory?

Krishnamurti: Sir, to observe and to listen, not only memory is necessary, but there must also be freedom from the known, from the memory. The question of memory is quite a complex problem. When is memory to function—completely, logically and sanely—and when must memory be quiet in order to look, to listen? One has to learn about this. But not in terms of time as you would learn a language—that demands time—but to learn by watching and listening to find out when memory, which is part of the brain, must respond instantly, healthily and with logic, and when the past, which is tradition, which is the conditioning, must be completely still so that one can look at the present in all its immensity, without the past. Can I look at myself as though I am seeing myself for the first time? Can I look at my wife, or my husband, or a tree or the running waters, as though I am looking with eyes that have never seen them before? This is not a romantic question, because if I look with all the memories, the images, the hurts, the fears, the pleasures and the hopes, then I am incapable of looking with eyes that are fresh, young and innocent. As we said before, innocency is love. Memory is not love because it is of the past. Memory is attachment to pleasure and to pain. But love is not of time, it has nothing to do with yesterday or tomorrow.

Q: Observation often brings thought into action. That is the difficulty.

K: If I may ask, did you listen to what was said previously before you asked the question?

Q: Yes.

K: You know, madam, it is one of the most difficult things to ask questions. We must ask questions, but also we must know when not to question but to listen. One must have doubts, scepticism, but also one has to tether that scepticism, when necessary. When the question is asked about the very act of thinking being action, that brings the question: what is action? Do you want to go into all this? Or are you tired after this morning?

Audience: No.

K: If you have really worked for forty-five minutes and followed what has been said about meditation, your brains must obviously be rather tired, because you have been giving a great deal of attention, which is rather difficult.

Q: Sir, you said that attention didn't use up energy.

K: Wait, madam. Did I say that attention doesn't use up energy? Go slowly. When attention is not effort it increases energy. If you have listened attentively, you have abundance of energy now and therefore you are not tired. Is that so? I can't answer for you.

We are asking what action is. Action means the active present. Please go into it semantically a bit. Action means the doing now, not having done or what you will do. If action is based on an ideal, or on a hope, or on a belief, it is no longer the active present, is it? I believe in something and I am acting according to that belief, principle or conclusion; therefore there is a division between the act and what the act should be; therefore it is not action. Or I will act according to my past experience, according to what I have learnt yesterday; then that is not action.

So one has to find out if there is an action that has no reference to the future or to the past. That, surely, is living. If I love my wife or my husband or my neighbour according to a conclusion, which has been part of my conditioning as a Christian, or whatever it is, then surely that act is not love. In the active present, the acting is the living, not the future or the past. If that living is based on past memory, then I am living in the past, and if that living is conditioned by the future because I have a formula or a conclusion or an ideal, then I am living in the future and not in the present. So can the mind, including the brain, live in the present, which is to act?

Q: I am thinking of people who are suffering physical illness. Can meditation bring about a process of healing?

K: Most of us have had pain of some kind, intense, superficial, or pain that cannot be cured. What effect has pain on the psyche, the brain or the mind? Can the mind meditate, dissociating itself from pain? Can the mind look at physical pain and observe it without identifying itself with that pain? If it can observe without identifying itself, then there is quite a different quality to that pain. I do not know if you have observed that if one has a toothache or stomach-ache, one can somewhat dissociate oneself from it. One does not have to rush to the doctor or take some pill; one observes it with detachment, with a feeling of looking at it as though one were outside it. Surely that helps the pain, doesn't it? The more you are attached to the pain, the more intense it is. So that may help to bring about this healing, which is an important question and which can only take place when there is no 'me', no ego or self-centred activity. Some people have a gift for it. Others come upon it because there is no ego functioning.

Q: I would like to know how you organized this conference without thinking about the future?

K: We said thought is necessary. We have to think about the future, about what we are going to do, how to organize the meetings in the tent and so on. Unless you think about the future, when you have to go home you will be in a state of amnesia, and you cannot possibly live that way. We have to think sanely and organize wisely for the future. But we are saying, when action is wholly conditioned by the past or by the future, then conflict comes out of that action. In organizing these meetings and planning for the School, we must use our thoughts very carefully and wisely, not bringing in our personal idiosyncrasies and characteristics, but by observing help to bring it about. If I stick to my opinion that it should be this way or that way, then there is no co-operation. Co-operation is only possible when there is no personal evaluation or personal idiosyncrasy interfering with the act.

Will you be any wiser when you leave here, any different, so that your whole mind and body are entirely awake and alert? Are we learning to look at the beauty of a tree, the flight of a bird, to watch a young child playing? Or are we going to step back into our shoddy lives with our particular characteristics, opinions, hopes and fears?

Q: May I ask if we are only the result of our past or can we be affected in some way by our future?

K: When we are violent and angry, that violence is part of the animal. We have evolved with the higher apes, we have got that violence in us. Aren't you the result of yesterday?

Q: Yes, we are. What I want to know is if this is all we are.

K: I call myself a Hindu; I am not, but that's what I call myself, and that has conditioned me: the climate, the food, the belief, the temples, the scriptures, the tradition. And through that conditioning, through the past, there runs a thread, a hope, a glimmer that wants to find out, go beyond the past. And the past projects the tomorrow, the future, doesn't it? The past is always incarnating in the future, modified, changing a little here and there. It is not a question of whether one is entirely of the past; of course one is not entirely the past as there is always modification going on. The past meeting the present modifies itself and thereby creates the future; but it is still the past, though somewhat changed. That is the whole cycle of reincarnation, the past everlastingly being reborn tomorrow. To change this process, this chain in which the mind is caught, is to understand and to be free of the past and the future. It is to understand one's own conditioning, the nationalism, and all the rest of it. And can one be free of it instantly, without taking time? That means not to be reborn again tomorrow.

Q: Sir, have we been conditioned to believe that we have a spirit or soul?

K: You know, there is a whole section, the Communists, who do not believe in spirit or in a soul. The whole Asiatic world believes that there is a soul, that there is the Atman. You can be conditioned to believe anything. The Communist doesn't believe in God; the others believe in God because that is the way they have been brought up. The Hindus believe in a thousand different gods, conditioned by their own fears, their own demands and their own urges. Can one become aware of these conditionings, not only of the superficial conditionings but also of those deep down, and be free of them? If one is not free, one is a slave, always living in this rat race; and that we call living.

Q: Can you avoid being affected by other people's fears when they react to you, when you have no fear of them yourself? Can one keep one's mind quiet and not be affected?

K: If I am not afraid, will you affect me? If I am not greedy, no amount of propaganda will affect me. If I am not nationalistic, all the waving of flags has no meaning. But going into it more deeply, the question can be asked: can the mind, which is the result of time and influence, be free of time and influence? Can I look at the newspaper and not be influenced? Can I live with my wife or my husband who wants to dominate me, and not be dominated? Can education be a process, not of influence, but a freeing from all

49

influence, so that the mind can think clearly and without confusion? But children want to be like others. All the movements of Hitler and Mussolini were based on influencing people to imitate each other and conform to the pattern. Although one is, of course, superficially influenced, which is a very small affair, can one live deeply without being really influenced at all? That can only take place when one sees things very clearly. It is only a confused mind that chooses, not the mind that sees very clearly.

14th September 1969

LISTENING WITHOUT CONCLUSIONS

Krishnamurti: This is supposed to be a dialogue, an exchange not merely of ideas but of our problems, in order to see if we can understand them and resolve them. There must be freedom between us to express whatever you want and freedom to listen, not be so occupied with our own problems that we refuse or don't have the patience to listen to others. So in order to communicate with each other, there must be freedom, patience, and a sense of deep, inward demand to comprehend, to understand. And also we must be able to face our problems, not merely remain at the intellectual, verbal level, but go into them very deeply in this exchange of our feelings, our ideas, our opinions, and expose ourselves, if we can, to each other, which is rather difficult. Otherwise I am afraid these discussions will have very little meaning. Can we talk with each other at that level freely, with an intention to inquire into ourselves and our problems and difficulties, and have the patience to listen to what others are saying? Also, can we change our opinions, our conclusions? Can we proceed along those lines?

Questioner: To observe the process of duality, does the mind function as a mirror to observe the observer?

K: Is that one of the questions we would like to discuss? Perhaps if we put half-a-dozen questions together, we might find the central issue which will cover all the other questions.

Can the mind observe the observer as in a mirror? Because the observer brings about this contradiction, this space between the observer and the observed, this duality, this conflict, this struggle. To understand the nature of the conflict, is it possible for the mind to observe the observer who brings about this dual existence as the 'me' and the 'not-me', both outwardly and inwardly?

Q: Could we look into the concern of people who think and feel that life has to have meaning?

Q: Thought appears to be quite separate. If one can become aware of what is happening in thought, it appears to be separate from the observer.

Q: Could we discuss what it means to bring the observer deeply within?

Q: Sir, could we also discuss this question of energy? It seems to me that we fritter away what little energy we do have in various automatic habits.

Q: Could we talk about the use of drugs as a means of coming upon self-awareness? So much of youth is involved in that now.

Q: One more question. When some characteristic response comes up in me and I go into it as deeply, as thoroughly as I can, for the time being it dissolves or goes away. Is this really observation that's been going on? If it comes back, is the problem really solved, or is it there within me all the time?

Q: Must one go through some psychotherapy first? Does one have to have some clarity before one can go on to deal with the problem of duality? Must one be at a certain point of health?

K: I think we have had enough questions. All right, let's take that question, shall we? Perhaps if we take that we can cover all the others.

Must I be in perfect health, or fairly good health, in order to observe myself? That means, if I am sick I cannot look at myself. And there is always some kind of trouble physically—tummyache, headache, overtiredness, friction, strain, eating unhealthy food and so on. There is always a little trouble going on all the time, one isn't in perfect health forever. That would be nice if it were possible, but it isn't.

Q: Sir, isn't a great deal of this due to our not giving these small ills attention, because we let our imagination dwell on them and they become much larger than they really are?

K: I'm just finding out whether a sick person, who is battling physically, has the energy to look at himself. We are not desperately ill, but we are not in the best of health; we are always slightly on the verge of being ill. Will such a state allow me to look at myself? Or is that slight ill health going to become a barrier to looking at myself?

Say I have a headache today. Will that prevent me from looking at myself? Obviously not. I can look at myself although I have a headache. I can look at myself although I am exhausted; I can watch myself very carefully, I am tired but I am watching. Physically I may be somewhat ill and perhaps in that state I can watch myself, but if I am not balanced psychologically as well as physically, if I am not really healthy psychosomatically, can I look at myself then? That is the real question, isn't it?

Q: We are often considerably unbalanced.

K: Yes, we'll go into that a little bit more slowly.

Q: In order to look at yourself, mustn't you be rid of all worry? Mustn't you cut yourself off from the world, its troubles and your troubles? If you have worries you won't be able to look at yourself.

K: You are saying, are you, that one must completely retire from the world? That is, withdraw completely and look at oneself. Is that possible? How do you discover what you are? Only in relationship, in communication with another.

Q: If we do have worries, I think it will be a lot harder.

K: Then I have to watch my worries, how they come about, whether they are self-created or being imposed, and so on. I have to inquire into that. But to say I must withdraw from all worry and then look at myself, that is impossible. Even if you withdrew into a monastery or became a beggar wandering about, as is done in India, you would still be in communication with others.

So the question really is, if one is physically not too unwell, then one can watch oneself, but if one is slightly neurotic, psychosomatically ill, that is, the mind affecting the body and the body affecting the mind, in that state is it possible to watch oneself? I hope we are communicating with each other. Can I look at myself through a distortion, through a psychosomatic disturbance? If it is very superficial I can, but if it is very deep I cannot.

Q: What about meditative love, won't that shoot through everything, make everything clear?

K: I do not know what we mean by meditative love. I am not being supercilious, but how do I know what meditative love is? I do not even know what love is, because I am in conflict. I am disturbed, I am anxious, I have got this neurotic state of mind, so I do not see things clearly. I completely believe in something and therefore it brings about imbalance in myself. How can I have this love and meditate, when there is all this confusion in me?

So, being somewhat neurotic, can I look at myself? Will my neurosis allow me to look at myself? If it is very deep, mustn't I have therapy, both physical as well as psychological? Mustn't I go to an analyst and through therapy begin to discover myself? This is really quite a deep problem for human beings.

I find out myself, or somebody tells me, that I am neurotic. I cannot think clearly, I cannot see things clearly, I am confused, I am miserable. I try to be something and I am not. I am battling in myself, I want to be so many things I cannot be. I want love, I want companionship, somebody to understand me. And I know I am slightly, or deeply, unbalanced. If I know I am neurotic, that I don't see things clearly, then there is some chance. But if I don't know that I am unbalanced, when I think I am positively right in my opinions, in my conclusions, in my outlook, then there is very little chance. Then perhaps one may have to go to an analyst and go through all that misery.

I have been wounded in my youth, perhaps sexually, emotionally, and that wound remains. It predominates over everything else. It shapes my outlook, and the memory of all that is so strong that it throws everything out of line. Then what am I to do with that wound, which may have been inflicted by the family, by the father, the mother, the environment? How am I to be rid of that memory, that conditioning?

Q: Not only that, sir, I can't find the memory.

K: Therefore, if I cannot find the memory what am I to do?

Q: Or I mistake it, I am looking at the wrong thing.

K: Yes, I may look at the wrong thing. I don't know what has wounded me or what has disturbed me, why I am like this. I have lived for many years, I've taken to drink, I've taken to drugs, I've been analysed for the last ten years, spent enormous sums of money. Everybody has been trying to help me out of this conditioning, then what am I to do?

Q: You have to live in the present, absolutely.

K: Madam, how can I live in the present? Please put yourself in that position.

We are all fairly neurotic in one way or another and we may not know it. When I do know that I am slightly, or deeply unbalanced, can I be aware of it? Can I see that I am unbalanced, sexually, physically, emotionally? I believe something and I fight, I resist everybody who questions that belief, and so on. Can I become aware, or must you show it to me? Am I willing to look at it? If you say, 'My dear friend you are neurotic, watch it', can I listen to you? Or do I say, 'You're not good enough, you are prejudiced, I cannot listen to you, I must go to a doctor, a specialist'?

Q: It seems to me, that the really essential factor in psycho-therapy is not the knowledge or experience of the analyst, but the freedom which exists in that relationship.

K: That is the question, isn't it? Freedom. Am I free to listen or am I resisting?

Q: If you are free to listen you have already made a step.

K: Quite right, I am already out, I am breaking through. But if I don't listen, what happens then?

Q: What about drugs? Would that help?

K: Would a drug help me to look at myself, to look at my fear, at my neurosis? Or would the drug give me an artificial experience?

Q: Sometimes that experience helps you to look at yourself.

K: Therefore I depend on the drug.

Q: You don't have to.

K: Wait, I take the drug, LSD or whatever it is, and it helps me to watch myself. And the watching fades away; I cannot watch myself all the time, all my old conditioning comes up and prevents me from looking because I'm afraid to look at myself. The drug may help me to quieten that fear, so that I can look. But the fear is there.

Q: The fear is there, but sometimes it is an unknown fear and the drug brings it out into the air.

K: Yes, sir, that is what we are saying. Sometimes it may help one to bring it out. But surely that's not good enough. I can take a drink sometimes and become relaxed. All my conditioning breaks down. But that doesn't last long.

Q: After the drug has worn off, you would forget everything, wouldn't you? Would you forget what you had learnt while you were under the drug?

K: Probably not. I don't know if you have taken it, I have not. I feel that to depend on something for perception, chemically or through repetition of words or drink and so on, indicates that there is fear. And that fear is exaggerated, sustained by dependence.

Q: We talk about drugs, but I think that we don't have a clear idea what we mean. I think that we have prejudices. We say that *this* is a drug, and *that* we call natural but

57

anything that we reach out for in order to change, in order to become more sensitive, we can look at as a drug.

K: Sir, I don't know if you have ever fasted just for the fun of it. If you have, it gives you a certain perception, you become much clearer if you do it only for a few days. Not if you do it for forty days, then it becomes much more difficult, then it is quite a different problem. If you have fasted for a few days, it makes the body extraordinarily sensitive, alert, watchful. And will you keep that up, will you fast every two weeks in order to watch yourself all the time, to become more alert?

Q: Sir, the drug is supposed to be a kind of vehicle to take you to yourself through all your inhibitions, your fears and all the things that keep you from knowing yourself. If you got to know your fears, which you don't with drugs, and finally reached yourself, wouldn't you know yourself a bit more? You understand better, if you understand what is blocking you.

K: This person was saying just now, that we are prejudiced against drugs. Do you think this is so?

Q: Isn't he saying that if you come to a perception of yourself without drugs that it has a more lasting effect?

K: That is what we are saying. Put it in any way you like. Take what is much simpler and more direct: I am in relationship with my wife or with my friend, why can't I use that relationship to watch myself? Why should I take a drug? There is my life right in front of me, every minute that I am living in relationship.

Q: But you said before that we're neurotic.

K: Wait a minute. I am neurotic. Why should I take a drug when there is a much more direct, simpler way of looking at myself, which is in my relationship? Will drugs help me to get over my neurosis? For the time being you are saying, it might help.

Q: It might take you a step ahead so that you can stop taking drugs and then continue without them.

K: I understand this. So you are saying, take them for a while, take them once, so as to get over the first step?

Q: Maybe.

K: I really don't know.

Q: But relationship only goes so far, then it gets blocked.

K: Must I use all these means, take drugs, or do something else? If I have no drugs, what shall I do to look at myself?

Q: I think that life itself is the only means. If this includes what we call drugs or anything else, it is still life and it is still the only means we have of looking at ourselves.

K: Then I use everything that you call life.

Q: If you exclude anything, then what you are doing is just excluding.

K: No, no, I am not excluding. I don't say I will never take drugs. There are ways of escaping from oneself: drugs, entertainment, cinemas, books, all kinds of things which are part of life. I don't exclude drugs, I don't exclude sex, I don't exclude anything, but I say, let's find out if there is not a simpler way.

Q: Surely, sir, speaking for myself, and I think for most of us, one of the dangers of drugs, or a religion, or a technique, is that we begin to depend on them, and the more we go on, the more we depend on them.

K: Yes, so let's come back to the point. Here I am, slightly unbalanced, and either I know it or I don't know it. If I know it, I can deal with it. If I don't know it, what am I to do?

Q: If I know it can I deal with it?

Q: If I don't know it, can I deal with it?

K: If I don't know that I am slightly off balance, if I won't listen to anybody, that is part of my neurotic state, what am I to do? I then begin to suffer. If it is a very bad neurosis, then I have a very bad time. That is one thing. But if I know it, then my problem is quite different. Shall I take drugs, or have psychoanalysis?

Q: Someone like this is very dependent on other people.

K: Yes. So what am I to do?

Q: Well, I think that when we learn something, when we know something, then it is changed.

K: Not quite so easy, sir. I know I dislike people, that is part of my neurosis. I have been hurt by people, they have brutalized me, at school, through sex, in ten different ways. They have made me brutal. I know I am a hard, cruel entity; I know it, but I can't get rid of it by knowing it. Then I want to find out how to get rid of it, how to become fairly quiet and gentle. What am I to do when I know that I am neurotic? That is the question we are discussing. Can I undo all the damage that has been done to me?

Q: You mentioned suffering, sir, and it seems to me that for many people that becomes a central issue because they struggle to get out of the suffering.

K: Yes, sir, that is so. We are putting the same thing in different words, aren't we? The conflict, the pain, the confusion, the misery—I know I am neurotic. The seed is there, which is producing all these things. So how am I to be rid of it?

Q: You've often spoken of the need to see that we must change totally. And you've also spoken of the fact that we have to look at ourselves without wanting to change what we see. Isn't there some kind of contradiction there?

K: Is there?

Q: To me there is, I don't fully understand that.

K: Can I look at one thing so completely that everything is included in that? Wait, sir, let's go slowly. I am aware that I am neurotic, and I know the cause of this imbalance. Merely knowing it doesn't resolve it, I go on being neurotic. Now what am I to do? It's like a compulsive eater who has to eat enormous quantities all the time. He knows he is compulsive, people have told him to watch it, but he goes on.

Q: It seems to have momentum. If there is something that gives it a momentum, it's hard to stop.

K: Sir, let's try this. Each one of us must know his own particular kink. Knowing it, let us see if the understanding of the cause which has brought it about will end it.

Q: Do we really understand the cause of it? We see a superficial cause and we think we see *the* cause.

K: There are ten different causes, maybe.

Q: Do we understand the purpose of what we do, not the cause, but the purpose of the neurosis, of our behaviour, of our hatred, and so forth?

Q: The psychologists say that if we know it only intellectually, not dynamically, we haven't really seen it.

K: That's the point. We say, 'I know it, I know the cause of it', but it is one of the most difficult things to say that one cause has produced it. There may be many different causes. Also, there is something much more involved in this: whether it is cause and effect. Let's not go into that for the moment because cause and effect is so definite: the cause becomes the effect, and the effect becomes the cause. This goes on all the time; that is quite a different matter. Let's look at this. Knowing the cause, in the sense of knowing merely intellectually, can I dissolve it? I say I can't. I have to find a way of dissolving it completely. What is that?

Q: Don't we have to look at it in action?

K: I feel angry, violent, and I hit you. Must I go to that extent?

Q: No, but one knows that if one looks at anger at the time, the anger dissolves.

K: Yes. Sir, our question is, mere knowing of the cause and the effect doesn't dissolve it. Therefore, as that person put it, I must enter into it, I must have tremendous feeling about it. I haven't got the feeling, so what am I to do? I can see intellectually why I am in this state and there I stop. How am I to feel this thing so strongly that I do something about it?

Q: In psychotherapy, ideally one forms a relationship that goes inside of it, because somebody else is going inside it with you.

K: Yes. You mean someone else is helping you to go into yourself, into this whole problem? Whether it is the guru, or the psychoanalyst, or your friend, then someone else is helping you. Now wait a minute, sir, isn't that what is being done now? Don't call it group therapy. Isn't that what is going on now?

Q: By now, you mean here?

K: Here. You tell me that I am neurotic and I listen to you. I say, 'Yes, you are perfectly right, I know it intellectually'. And you say, 'Don't look at it intellectually, let's go into it together more deeply, emotionally, dynamically, and feel it'. You are helping me but I reach a point where you cannot help me any more.

Q: Sir, must one not do away with aids and escapes to start with? They must be out of the way.

K: Now I've reached the point when I see I must tackle it deep down, in the sense that I must feel it with all my heart, with my whole being. You have helped me to come to that point. After that I have to do it myself.

Q: One feels one often lacks the energy.

K: Wait a minute, we are just coming to that. You have helped me to watch myself. You have helped me to be aware of my neurosis. Together we have gone into this up to a certain point. All that has required energy and attention. I've listened to you because I really want to solve this problem. It is a tremendous burden for me; I can't get on with people; I am miserable and unhappy. And you have helped me to come to that point, first intellectually, then a little more deeply. Now I am there and you can't help me any more. Can you help me to go much deeper or can you only help me up to a certain point?

Q: How do I know I have reached this point?

K: I've tried, I've experimented, I've tested.

Q: It can be of tremendous value to be helped up to that point.

K: Granted.

Q: Our questions may be part of the trouble. Perhaps it is because we start out with the idea of someone helping us.

K: I'm coming to that, madam, you'll see it in a minute. What is involved in this question is that you have helped me up to a point.

Q: Sir, once this person has helped you, is there a danger that you might be dependent on him and you don't really feel it yourself?

K: I am questioning the whole method, sir. I am saying to myself that you are supposed to have helped me, that you have led me. We have walked together up to a certain point.

Q: But then won't you be dependent on me when we get to this point?

K: Why can't I realize this at the very beginning? Why should I go through all this to come to that point?

Q: No one in the world can help you all the way.

K: Don't say that! You have helped me to realize that you cannot help me. Do see that point, sir. Please have the patience. We have walked together and you have pointed out the dangers. You have shown my states to me very clearly, both verbally and non-verbally. You have held my hand, you have done everything. And I say that's very little; it helps only to a certain degree. So suddenly I realize: why should I have your help at all? Why can't I do this myself right from the beginning?

Q: But if one sees that, then one has reached a certain intelligence.

K: Therefore, what does that mean? Can I see that point in my neurotic state? A dozen things are offered—drugs, analysis, sunshine, group therapy, individual therapy, sitting together for twenty-four hours, feeling more sensitive by touching each other, touching the grass. People do all these things. Some people may say they need all that. If you want to do that, all right, but I am asking myself if I must go through all this. Must I touch you to become sensitive, go to college to become sensitive? I overeat, indulge sexually, do all kinds of things in order to destroy my sensitivity, and then I take a drug to become sensitive. It's crazy. Therefore I am asking myself how I am to become extraordinarily alert to my own neurotic state. What will give me the energy, the drive, the intensity to go through it myself right from the beginning?

Q: Maybe the crisis can't solve itself, but it seems to reach a crisis of its own accord. Does that mean anything?

K: Crisis means a shock, sir, a challenge, something that demands your attention. A crisis is only possible when there is a challenge. And if you respond to it actively, adequately, the crisis is not a crisis. But I cannot because I am weak.

Q: Doesn't the very wanting to do it give you the energy?

K: The very want is a waste of energy. Wait, can we discuss for the moment how to bring about energy, how to bring all the energy into this?

Q: Looking at the unhappiness in the world and the passionate desire to understand myself brings the energy.

K: I haven't the desire, I want to escape from myself.

65

Q: Yes, that is the point.

K: Sir, the whole world is helping me to escape from myself. The religions, the books, the philosophers, the analysts, everybody says, 'Run away, for God's sake don't look'. And you say I must have the desire. How does this desire come? Desire is greater sensation. I desire that in looking at myself I'll have greater pleasure; otherwise I won't have desire. If there is no reward, why should I have a desire?

Q: Is it possible to be in pain and not desire to be out of pain?

K: Sir, if you have a toothache, it is a natural thing to get rid of it, isn't it? And sometimes you can't. If you have a headache, or whatever it is, you take aspirin, and if it goes on what do you do then?

Q: You just suffer the pain. You just suffer.

K: Wait. Don't say, 'Just suffer'. If you identify yourself with the suffering, there is conflict, isn't there? You say, 'I'll watch the pain', unless it is unbearable, and then I either lose consciousness or take some drug. But if it is not so violently painful, I can watch it. There is no identifying with the pain, no saying that I must get rid of it, that I must fight it, resist it.

Q: Is acceptance resistance?

K: Sir, if a dog is barking all the time some night and you cannot do anything about it, have you ever noticed what you do? Do you resist it?

Q: Often.

K: What happens then? You are fighting it and you become more and more awake.

Q: Can't one go the other way round so that one becomes more relaxed?

K: So what do you do?

Q: You can listen to it.

K: Which means what? Don't resist it, listen to it. Don't fight it, go with it. In India, it happens often that a dog barks for hours. Either you fight it or you go with it, join it. In the same way, when there is great pain, unless it is unbearable, I go with it. There is no resistance, no saying, 'I must get rid of it immediately'.

So we come to the point: how can I have the vitality, the energy to make me observe so intensely?

Q: I think that if something is important enough to the peace of mind, the security, the well-being of the brain, then the energy is concentrated there, but if it is not important enough there will be no energy.

K: So you are saying, sir, that if the thing is important enough, there is the energy.

Q: But all I know is, one has only to observe it to get over it.

K: Before you say that, there is another question. If you are interested in getting rid of, or trying to understand fear, then you have the energy. That is what you are saying. But if I am not interested?

Q: I didn't say interested. I didn't say intellectual interest.

K: No, sir, that is what I mean. How do you bring about this vital interest to face fear? Someone says to take a drug or do various things that will help you to look, to be really involved in it.

Q: I come to a point where my mind puts the fear into words. And I see that even my mind is a sort of analyst.

K: Quite.

Q: It cannot help me further.

K: So the question now is: how do I have enough energy? I need energy to look at myself when I am neurotic, unbalanced, afraid, whatever it is.

Q: May I ask why, sir? I don't quite see why we need energy to look?

K: Energy means attention, doesn't it? (Sound of aeroplane.) There is an aeroplane. To listen to it completely without any resistance is attention, isn't it? Otherwise I will resist it, I will say, 'I won't listen to it, I want to hear what is being said'. But to listen to that noise completely you need attention, which is energy focused to listen. It doesn't matter, use any other word.

Q: I mean, does it use up energy?

K: No, on the contrary. It is only when I resist it, when I am inattentive, that I lose energy. If I listen to that aeroplane wholly, I have much more energy. The inattention wastes energy.

Q: And the attention brings energy.

K: It *is* energy. It doesn't get dissipated; on the contrary, it builds up more and more.

Q: I see that, sir. Before, it sounded as though you were saying that you must find a lot of energy before you can look.

K: No, on the contrary. So can I attend completely in order to observe? Then the problem arises, is the observer different from the thing observed? This was a question raised at the beginning. If there is attention, all the energy focused in looking, is there an observer? If there is an observer, then there is inattention, because the observer resists. He has got his prejudices, his opinions. He says, 'This is good, I'll keep it, but I don't want that'. He is fighting to gain pleasure, to avoid pain. He is avoiding or accumulating, and that is a dissipation of energy. Can I attend without the observer? I will do it when I actually see the truth that it is a waste of energy to look with the observer.

Can I listen to you freely, without opinions or conclusions, without saying you're right, just listen? Can I listen to that aeroplane freely? When you tell me I am a fool, can I listen to you without reacting? The reaction is the observer.

Q: Then in that state does the mind function as a mirror?

K: Is the mind then like a mirror that only reflects? Surely it is not reflecting? When it looks at the tree, the tree is not imprinted on the mirror.

So what have I learnt this morning? I have learnt—I *am learning* rather—that, deeply, nobody can help me. That is a tremendous realization. Whoever wants to help me, is helping me according to his conditioning. He says, 'I know better than you do, let me help you'; or, 'I'll be a companion, we'll walk together, we'll watch things together'. Which means that I depend on him, that I need someone to support me in walking. And I have discovered that if ultimately I have to do something myself, why not start right from the beginning. I can't do it if I am frightened, or want support, security, want somebody to tell me. And I have seen that any form of resistance, outwardly or inwardly, is a waste of energy. When I have an opinion about something or other, and I am unwilling to change it, that is a resistance. When you say something, giving your opinion, can I listen to it without resisting, and change my mind when what you say is true? Can I cease to have opinions at all?

I see that where there is attention there is abundance of energy. That energy is attention, and it can look and observe without the observer. The observer is the conditioned entity, the reaction, the resistance. I have seen this very clearly, not intellectually but deeply. I feel it. Therefore I am going to watch if there is any form of resistance creeping up, and I know what to do. Now I am free to listen, and therefore free all the time, changing.

9th September 1969

ASKING THE RIGHT QUESTION

Krishnamurti: What shall we talk over together?

Questioner: Can we discuss how craving sustains conditioning?

Q: The non-dualistic nature of the mind.

Q: The problem of change.

Q: Sir, you spoke about energy and you said attention was energy and that it did not use up energy. I don't understand that.

Q: The question of seeing, the difference between seeing and recognizing a description of one's mental structure.

K: Could we approach all these questions by inquiring into what we mean by learning? I am just suggesting, I am not pushing this forward as my particular question. Perhaps we could then understand conditioning and the attention of awareness which does not waste energy, and so on. Could we begin there and then bring all the questions into that?

Here is a question, put at the beginning: craving strengthens conditioning. And any form of resistance, contradiction, opposing desires, are a waste of energy, because in that there is involved a great deal of effort, struggle, frustration and fear. All that is a waste of energy. Could we learn about it? Not be told what to do, or how to think, or how not to waste energy, but learn together about this: craving strengthens one's conditioning and any form of resistance is a waste of energy. And what do we mean by learning? Can we approach it that way? Would that be worthwhile? Instead of my telling you what it is and you telling me what it is, can't we learn about it?

71

What does learning mean? Not only at the school level, at the university level, or the technological level, but also learning through experience. In this is involved testing, going through a particular form of experience and learning from it, and utilizing what one has learnt as a means of testing. So I think it might be worthwhile to find out what we mean by learning. It is really quite a complex problem; it needs a great deal of inquiring into, thinking about or, perhaps more, *feeling* your way into it.

Now here is a statement: resistance is a waste of energy. I hear that and I want to find out the truth of it or the falseness of it. I want to learn about it. I don't accept it, I don't reject it; I want to find out. First of all, there is a great deal of curiosity about that statement and whether there is a fragment of truth in it, or anything that is worthwhile, which can be tested, learnt about, experienced and lived. When I hear such a statement, I am really quite curious, like a schoolboy who wants to know and who asks many questions.

Q: Sir, I think curiosity is one of the essential ingredients of learning, because otherwise you are forcing yourself to do something.

K: Quite, otherwise it becomes mechanical, mere cultivation of memory. So we say curiosity is necessary. Now wait a minute. Am I curious? Not about how you live or what you do, what you think, which becomes gossip, interference, impudence. That is not curiosity, that is ugly. I am curious to find out for myself whether that statement has any meaning for me at all. When there is curiosity, there is energy, isn't there? I am really excited about it, I am not casual about it. I am not indifferent, I am really curious, and that curiosity gives me an impetus, a drive to find out.

Q: In fact we have to consider the motive of the curiosity.

K: I am curious, there is no motive. If there is a motive, there is no curiosity. I want to learn because I am curious. If it is in order to gain more money, that is not curiosity; the motive then is much more important, more vital than curiosity itself. Am I curious without a motive? I want to find out. I recognize that in myself there is no motive. I just want to learn whether the statement that resistance is a waste of energy is true or false. So I say to myself: 'Do I resist anything, psychologically as well as physically?' It is quite interesting if you really go into it. Shall we?

Please bear in mind that I have no motive, I just want to find out, I am curious. When a first-class scientist is exploring, he is not driven by a motive. A person who has a motive that he might achieve great fame and money and all the rest of it is not a scientist. He is just like anybody else, using science for his own benefit.

So I am just curious. There is no motive behind curiosity, that is a fact. I am talking about myself, not about you. Now I want to find out if I resist. I may resist a dozen things in life: my wife, the children, the boss, society, what somebody says to me. I am free to inquire, free to find out in what way I resist. Shall I examine this resistance in fragments? You understand what I mean—I resist here, there, and so on. I am taking that as an example. Shall I look at resistance as a fragmentary process? I resist you because what you say may be true, and I want to resist because I am frightened of you. I am frightened of not being able to sit on the platform. So shall I examine this statement applicable to myself, in myself, in fragments, or shall I be able to look at it, learn about it, as a whole?

73

Belief is a form of resistance. Would you say that? When I am a Hindu, or a Muslim or a Christian, there is a resistance against all other forms of belief, all other dogmas. I am a Communist and I reject everything else. Therefore I am resisting.

Q: So anything that impinges on the mind ...

K: Wait, we'll come to that presently. Go slowly step by step. Don't come to any conclusions. I have found that any form of conclusion is a resistance. I conclude that this is wrong and that is right; that is a conclusion and I resist what I consider wrong, and hold on to what I consider right. I resist my wife because she dominates me, or I resist any form of questioning because I may find myself in a state of uncertainty, which I dislike, which may invite fear. Therefore I resist.

So shall I look at these fragments of resistance and try to learn from each fragment, or can I look at this whole form of resistance and learn from it? Let's go together, otherwise it's no fun, at least for me.

Q: I don't see how this whole form of resistance expresses itself other than through lots of little resistances.

K: Yes, I quite agree. But I have put that question. Don't accept it, we are learning. I may be totally wrong. I say to myself, 'Shall I learn bit by bit, watch myself resisting any form of infringement on my freedom by society, by the priest, the government, or by my wife?' That is one form of resistance. And another form of resistance is belief; I am frightened that if I don't have that belief, something might happen to me. Shall I learn from each example or is it possible to learn about the whole of resistance, not bit by bit?

Q: Do you mean that there is a common reason at the back of every form of resistance?

K: No.

Q: Or a common factor, that it is caused by the same thing?

K: Look, I am resisting in various ways. My question would be: why am I resisting at all, what for? Not the reason for it, I want to see the fact that I am resisting. First I must know I am resisting. I am curious to find out if I am resisting. The moment I am aware that I am resisting, there is already the discovery of the cause. I am resisting you because I think I am much more intelligent, superior, more spiritual than you, and what you say might pull me down a little in front of the others, therefore I am going to resist you.

So I recognize I am resisting and I am learning about it. My mind is curious, and therefore I find out why I am resisting; not only you, but I see the whole of resistance. Are we going on together? Are you sure?

Audience: Yes.

K: I have formed an opinion, right or wrong, and I stick to it and I resist every other opinion. I believe in something and it is *my* knowledge, or others have informed me, and it strengthens my opinions. Now why do I have opinions at all? I recognize opinion is a form of resistance. Now I am going to learn, and with that sense of urgency and energy I find out why I am resisting altogether. Is not my whole life—please listen to this—a way of resistance? I think I am somebody, I have an image of myself and I don't want you to destroy that image. Or I have various forms of beliefs, dogmas, knowledge, experiences, which have given me a certain vitality, strength and technique to tackle life, and I am going to resist everything else. So I say to myself, 'I see this very clearly. I have found out that my whole life is a form of resistance'. Please, I am only communicating with you; don't agree or disagree.

Q: You mean it is a selection of one set of possibilities as against another?

K: Yes.

Q: And therefore you are resisting the others. And that forms your particular character.

K: That's right. The Greek word for character comes from "engrave". Engraving on the mind is my character. My mind has been engraved upon and I have a particular character: strong, weak, purposive, direct, dominating, this or that. And the thing that has been engraved on my mind is going to continue, resisting everything else. So I am asking myself, 'Is my life a form of resistance, is living a form of resistance?'

Q: Yes, because with that resistance I build up my security. I feel secure in that and I am afraid to let it go.

K: Are you saying, madam, that resistance is a form of building up security? Is it? I am not saying it is not, I am just asking. I don't want to reduce it to one word. This is much too explosive; you cannot just say that one word explains everything.

Q: One of the things one might be resisting is embarrassment, or shame.

K: Of course, all that is implied. I don't want to examine each detail, but see this whole problem of resistance. Is my life based on resistance because I have an image of what I must be, what I should be, what I am, or what I want to achieve?

Q: What gives the energy, the force to this image that one has of oneself? Why is it so strongly engrained in the mind?

K: That is fairly simple, surely. Every form of influence is continually impinging on my mind: the family, society, my own desires.

Q: Isn't it that all these different resistances are a means of protecting this image, defending it?

K: Is that what you have found, madam? Is that what you have learnt?

Q: Yes. Sometimes.

K: Now you see what has happened? Curiosity has aroused tremendous energy in me to find out. And I am looking, watching where I am resisting. I want to learn, because I see—which is not a conclusion—that any form of experience is to be tested. Any form of resistance divides people, therefore there is no communication, no relationship; therefore there is conflict and no peace.

Q: Is not resistance the fear one has of the idea of death?

K: Yes. That is also included. So shall we go along? I hope you are all as intense about this as the speaker is, because I really want to find out if there is any form of resistance in me. I want to learn about the idea that I am a great man, about that image, the idea of success, of popularity, reputation, being a leader—all those horrors. Is the mind resisting anything? Which means the mind has taken a position with regard to politics, economy, religion, the family, and it is unwilling to move from there.

Q: When we speak of resistance, the mind starts resisting resistance.

K: Yes, and tradition is also a resistance. So I want to find out if I have a tradition.

There is that statement: craving strengthens conditioning. Does it? Why do I crave? I understand that I crave for food when I am hungry. There is the biological, sexual urge and the image that thought builds around that urge. There is craving for sexual excitement, or the craving for power, for position, or for peace. Is all that craving—the wanting, demanding, insisting? I am hungry, I need food. Is that craving, or is it the natural response of an organism that needs food? Would you call that craving? But craving does come when I say, 'I must have that particular kind of food which tastes better'. And there is the whole structure of sexual demands; the biological urge is different from the craving that thought creates about the urge. Are you following?

Q: Will you please repeat that last sentence?

K: The biological urge is strengthened by thought creating or building an image of all that. That becomes the craving.

Q: Are we afraid that if we don't crave we cease to live?

K: No, I don t say that. What does this craving mean? I am trying to inquire. There are natural, organic, biological urges and demands, and thought takes hold of them and transforms them into something called craving, appetites. Then thought says, 'I must be careful, because I am a respectable man, therefore I must be wise in my appetites'. So there is a battle going on between two thoughts. I don't know if you follow what I mean? There is the thought that has created the image, the picture of the sexual demands, and the thought that says, 'Be careful'. So thought forms a resistance against the thought which has created the pic-

78

ture, the sensation. So you see how resistance has been formed.

Q: But, sir, surely sometimes resistance might be necessary?

K: We are coming to that in a minute. First let's get the picture. So thought encourages in one direction and thought resists that. It says, 'I must resist, otherwise I may be destroyed—by society, by my wife, and so on—therefore it is good, it is wise, it is normal to resist'.

Q: The desire that is pushed on by thought leads in a direction that disturbs the temporary equilibrium. And the opposing thought tries to restore it at a different level. That's what I see.

K: That's right, sir. So I have learnt a great deal.

The mind is looking at itself to see whether there is any form of duality going on. Resistance is duality. There is opposition, contradiction, and in that there is conflict. Therefore I say to myself, 'The whole of resistance is a waste of energy'.

I've learnt that, it isn't that somebody else has told me. It isn't that the speaker on the platform has pointed it out and therefore I am repeating after him. It is something that I have actually learnt out of my curiosity, my energy and drive, not as an idea which I am going to apply, but as an actual fact. I see that resistance breeds duality and therefore conflict, which is essentially a waste of energy.

Now I am going to inquire where it is necessary to resist, or if one can live without any resistance at all. I want peace. God knows why, but I want it, I think it is marvellous to live in peace. You come along, because you have heard somebody say so, and tell me I can have peace if I do certain things—meditate, repeat words, listen to sound, sit this way, breathe that way, and so on. And I want that, because intellectually I can see that a mind that is very peaceful is extraordinarily alive, beautiful, has a certain vitality, intensity. So what you say appeals to me and I practise it and get certain experiences and a certain feeling, a certain quiet. I want peace, and I find peace can be had at a certain price and I am willing to pay for it. And I resist every other form of teaching.

I know all that. So I say to myself, 'Can I live completely, right through my whole being without resistance, not having to resist this or that, follow this person and not that person? Can I live that way, not theoretically but actually? Can I live my daily life without any resistance?' If you want my coat, shall I resist? If you want any of my property, will I yield and not resist you? If you say, 'Do this, think this way, don't think that way', shall I resist you? Where shall I yield and not yield? How can you tell me, or I tell you where to yield and where not to yield? Or have I to learn about it? If you tell me that I must yield here and not there, you have already set a resistance going in me. But I am going to find out for myself where I must yield without resistance, and where I must not yield. That means I shall find out how to act at a particular moment, but not come to that moment with a conclusion. If I come to that moment with a conclusion, I am already resisting. Because I have no principle (which is a conclusion), I have no ideology, and there is freedom. So I say to myself, 'I am learning, I have found the truth'. I have no opinion, no conclusion, there is no resistance. That perception has been made clear, and I say that every minute of the day I am going to find out.

Q: Isn't it that we are afraid of the energy?

K: The fear *is* energy. You cannot be afraid of a fear, fear is a form of energy. No?

Q: But it seems that one is constantly diverting energy into resistance or fear, or something else.

K: Look, I am afraid. I am going to learn about fear. I am not going to translate, saying it is a waste of energy, or it is energy, and so on. I have no conclusion about fear, and therefore I am free, curious to learn. So I am going to learn what fear is. It is a form of resistance, because I am afraid I might die tomorrow, or I am afraid of my father and mother.

Q: Is the fear of death unconsciously at the root of the whole of the resistance against every day?

K: Sir, are you afraid to go into the question of fear? Actually, deeply are you aware that you are afraid? Shall I resist fear by cultivating courage? A form of resistance is called courage. It isn't courage, it is a resistance. I am afraid, and I am escaping from it. Surely escape is resistance to what is. So I want to find out if I am escaping. There are so many ways of escape, let's not go into them. And what shall I do with fear? I am not escaping because I see that resistance doesn't dissolve fear, doesn't push it away.

Q: When I have seen that fear and resistance are only the fear of death, can I not realize, at least intellectually, that life and death are the same thing? At that moment the fear will vanish.

K: It is not quite like that, is it? I am not really interested in death. It is inevitable, it will come later. But I *am* really frightened of my wife. I'm sorry, I'll take something else! (Laughter.) Frightened of what, sir?

Q: Inadequate responses?

K: Let's take that. I am frightened of my incapacity to respond fully to life. And I am not resisting, I am not escaping, I am full of curiosity to find out why I am frightened because I can't respond fully. The fact is I can't. What am I frightened of?

Q: Because it's so uncomfortable to live with.

K: Which means what? I dislike living uncomfortably. Or I find that I cannot respond completely, adequately, because my mother and father beat me when I was a baby—you know the whole process of going back to childhood. So, am I frightened because of my inadequate response? All right, I'm inadequate, why should I be frightened of it? Because I have an image that I must respond fully, think that if I don't I will be unhappy, I'll be in conflict, I'll be miserable, uncomfortable and all the rest of it. Therefore I say I am inadequate, and this frightens me; therefore fear is a form of resistance. Do you get it? If I have no picture of what adequacy is, then I am just inadequate—all right.

Q: Is it not being aware of what is?

K: No, madam, listen to it a little bit. I haven't finished yet. I am inadequate. I have fear because I have an image that I should be adequate. But if I have no image, what tells me I am inadequate? Please, don't shrug it off.

Q: Comparison.

K: Quite right. Do please listen. He said, it is comparison. Why do I compare? That is my habit, isn't it, from childhood on through university and throughout life. I have always lived in a society, in a state of mind, that is continually comparing—a bigger car, a smaller car, more beautiful, less beautiful, more intelligent, less intelligent, more money, less money, and so on. You follow? Why am I comparing? I am curious, I am learning. You understand? I see comparison has caused inadequacy in me. If I don't compare there is no inadequacy. I am what I am. I may be stupid, but that is all right.

Q: But, sir, it's not always like that.

K: Of course; nothing is *always* like that.

Q: I mean, it is not always comparison that makes one feel inadequate.

K: I am examining comparison, madam. My life is comparative: I want peace, I am not peaceful. How do I know that I have not the idea of peace? So why do I compare? Please follow this. Can I live without comparison: the ideal, the hero, the bigger man, the lesser man, the inferior, the stupid? Can I live without any comparison, at any time?

Q: It seems to be the linguistic structure of thought that has comparison built in.

K: Quite so. In language itself there is comparison. Having seen that, I am not going to say I am more or I am less. The very structure of the 'me' is comparative.

Q: Don't we confuse comparative facts with comparative judgements?

K: Comparative facts such as, 'This colour is red, I prefer blue', 'I don't like this'—those are fairly clear. But I want to get my teeth into much deeper things than that; which is, can I live completely without comparison? Not the comparison of judgement such as, 'You are fairer than I am'; obviously I am brown and you are fair; so what? But I am asking myself, I am full of curiosity to find out, whether the mind can live without comparing. And is not the mind itself the result of comparison—the tall and the small, more and less? I can only live non-comparatively when I am absolutely looking at the fact and not what the fact should be or must not be.

Q: But, sir, take two facts side by side.

K: No, no, there is no such thing as two facts side by side. Look, there is one fact at a time, not two facts at one time.

Q: No, but it is a way of perceiving difference.

K: No, that is what that lady was saying just now.

Q: Not only in red and blue, but in many things, in people and objects.

K: Opinion, then.

Q: And events and so on.

K: No. madam, look, there is only one fact. A second later maybe there'll be another fact.

Q: And then we see the difference.

K: Yes, then what? What are you trying to say, madam?

Q: I am trying to say that one learns by seeing the difference about oneself. One only sees one thing in oneself, one doesn't see that there are other things. From time to time one compares and it is a way of learning.

K: Do please listen to what you are saying. Do I learn through comparison?

Q: We do learn.

K: Please find out, don't insist.

Q: We do, yes. I mean, I have found it out.

K: No, no, madam, that doesn't mean anything. Sorry, forgive me if I contradict you. Do I learn anything by comparing or do I only learn by looking at the fact and inquiring about that fact; not by comparing that fact with another fact? I have a Chinese vase and a Persian vase. By looking at the Chinese vase I learn all about it. But if I begin to compare the two, I am learning about something else, not about the fact of the Chinese vase.

Q: Krishnaji, but there are certain facts in relation to other facts. For instance, if you were considering the speed of something, you would learn it in relation to the speed of other things. That would be part of the fact, would it not? That's comparison.

K: You are saying you learn about that fact much quicker than I do.

Q: No, I am speaking of the objective relation of two facts. For instance, light has a different speed than a motor car. Those two are facts, and their relationship is a further fact. One has to consider the two things in order to learn something about them.

K: All right. A Mercedes goes much faster than a bullock cart. That is a fact and that doesn't touch me or interfere with my life.

Q: You learn about the speed by going in the bullock cart. When you are in the Mercedes you feel the speed of the Mercedes, there is no need to compare it with the bullock cart.

K: Wait a minute. Not only that, there is another fact involved. Do I learn by comparing myself with you, who learn much more quickly? There is speed involved in this too. You learn something extraordinarily quickly, you see very clearly. Immediately resistance arises and all the implications of it. Your perception is instantaneous, with mine I have to go little by little. You act much more quickly, my action is slower. Why am I comparing myself with you? Where does speed come into this, the more, the less? Why?

Q: Because of the images.

K: No, because I am envious of her. I want to have the same thing that she has, to be as quick as she is, because I have compared myself with her. That comparison is very fast. Why am I comparing myself? Can I live without being aware that you are much quicker than I am? Can I free myself linguistically from the comparative judgement about myself? Therefore, can I look at myself non-comparatively, non-verbally, for the word in itself is comparative?

I am really very curious and therefore full of delightful energy, to find out if I can live without comparison at all. Comparison implies pretension. There is a great deal of hypocrisy in comparison. I want to be like Christ, like the Buddha, the hero, and I am not. I am comparing myself with them and pretending, striving, struggling to be that. And I say, 'What nonsense'. I see that to live without comparison means complete honesty to oneself, not to anybody else. The moment I compare myself, I am pretending, putting on a mask. It is like being in school. If B is compared to A—as happens always, through examinations, in class, in every way—if you tell B he must be like A, you are destroying B. And that is the kind of education we have all had. So education becomes violent, destructive. Can we educate ourselves without comparing?

Q: Sir, we have to find out where comparison has its place, where it is necessary and where it isn't.

K: Of course, sir. That is what we said.

Q: How can we not be aware of the differences? We are aware of them.

K: Oh, no, on the contrary. We are saying, be aware of the contradiction. Contradiction exists when there is a resistance. We've been through all that.

Q: I cannot see my head, I just see this part of my body; how could I compare it with the whole body which I see everywhere?

K: I only know I have a head through comparison? (Laughter.) I look in a mirror.

Q: It wasn't a very good example, but we do learn about ourselves by seeing things around us, in other people. It's not always brought about by envy, it is observation.

K: No, madam.

Q: We can learn.

K: You are saying you can learn by watching others, in many ways. By watching the animal—its violence, its devotion, its pleasures—I learn, because I am part of the animal, my whole background is derived from the higher apes, and so on. At least that is what the scientists say. Others will say, 'No, you are straight from God'. Must I watch the animal to learn about myself? Must I watch you to learn about myself?

Q: It can be useful.

K: How can it be useful? Have I the eyes?

Q: But I am blind to myself.

K: Therefore you are blind to others.

Q: No, they can open up your eyes sometimes, in a flash.

K: They can wake you; every shock, every challenge, every question does wake you. But do I depend on questions, a challenge, looking at others, to keep awake?

Q: It is all part of it.

K: No, madam, part of me is asleep, therefore I am not awake. It is like the curate's egg. [A curate at the bishop's breakfast table was embarrassed to find his egg inedible. Asked by the bishop if his egg was bad, he replied, 'It is good in parts.']

Q: Is this form of comparison a desire to imitate?

K: Surely. Please, sir, don't take part of this and part of that, but find out whether you can live without comparison. Isn't that the only way to live? Doesn't that give you tremendous energy? But if I am comparing myself with the Prime Minister or with Jesus, or whatever it is, what a waste of life it is. So I am watching, I am learning about comparison, and therefore I know when comparison has its values and when it has no value at all.

Q: That is what I meant when I first said that it had some use.

K: No, forgive me again. We must start by saying, 'Can one live without comparison?' Not 'It helps sometimes and doesn't help at other times', 'Comparison is necessary', or 'Comparison is not necessary'. When the right question is asked, and answered rightly, then that will bring about the right response when comparison is necessary. But I must ask the right question, the fundamental question first. Can I live without comparison? Not 'on some days' or 'sometimes'; if I have answered that question, not verbally or intellectually, but deeply, totally, then I will know when it is necessary and when it is not necessary.

It is like knowing what co-operation is completely, deeply. Then only will you know when not to co-operate. But to say, 'Mustn't I co-operate with this and not co-operate with that, isn't it necessary sometimes?' leads to greater and greater confusion. When you know how to co-operate fundamentally—not around an idea, around a feeling, around an emotion, but to co-operate without any resistance—then you will also know very deeply, when not to co-operate. So one must ask the right question first.

September 11th 1969

Part Two

Shattering all Conditioning

Shattering all Conditioning

KRISHNAMURTI AND EDUCATION AT BROCKWOOD PARK SCHOOL

A Conversation with Mary Zimbalist and Mary Cadogan

Mary Cadogan: We thought perhaps to start this dialogue Mary and I would talk a little bit about the beginnings of the School, the history, the background. Some of you know this already but perhaps some of you don't, and we hope you'll forgive us any repetitions. We're talking quite informally and taking up various aspects of Krishnaji's approach to the schools. With this in mind we are going to go back quite a long way, and Mary will start.

Mary Zimbalist: It really goes back a very long way, as I discovered to my surprise in reading a little book by Krishnaji (as Alcyone) that was published in the early Theosophical days, called *Education as Service*. It's in the distant past; the only reason I mention it is to show that in 1912 he was already concerned with education. And later on, in talks to some of us, he said that he had been especially and very deeply concerned with education from 1925 when he started thinking about having schools. So this involvement really goes back to 1912 when he was seventeen years old. This shows that schools were essential to him from a very early time.

MC: Perhaps we can consider that it goes back to his own schooling, for he had a far from ideal pattern of schooldays. For much of these, as he says himself, he was dreamy—he even used the word "vacant", which I think in a sense must mean "very open" or "empty"—but obviously, as a very sensitive child, there were many things in his schooldays, which were pretty dreadful. I mean he was actually *beaten.*

MZ: Yes. It says in the Foreword to this little book—it may have been altered, but the Foreword was by him—that he had seen both the worst and the good in schools; and the worst for him was being beaten and put out on the porch where he was left for the rest of the day.

MC: And even forgotten.

MZ: Oh, yes.

MC: Although his brother remembered him and he took him home. So he did have a very unfortunate start with his own schooldays, and probably this led him to feel passionately about this. And certainly working with him, and knowing him, one felt that this concern with education in every aspect was always there. I think he started his first schools in India in the 1920s.

MZ: Well, I believe that he started a sort of a school, or maybe it was a study group, when he was still in his teens.

MC: I first got to know Krishnamurti in the early 1950s, and at that time there was some pressure for a school to begin in Europe, a Krishnamurti school. It was interesting to see how he responded to that. He listened very intently to the people who came forward with offers or wishes to start a school, parents, of course, and teachers. He seemed to take it all quite serenely but was not disposed to move quickly on it. He certainly seemed to feel it was terribly important to get the right people, the right place. And I felt he was also saying the right time, in the sense of the atmosphere being right. I remember something he said to me about the dancer Isadora Duncan. He knew I had an interest in her because I had taught a system of movement and dance which sprang partly from her work. Krishnaji said that she felt the greatest disaster in her life was starting a school! He actually quoted this to me and laughed. I read her autobiography later on, and indeed she does say this. But fortunately that was not the greatest disaster in Krishnamurti's life, although he obviously realized that starting a school wasn't something you jumped into without a great deal of care and looking into the situation. So for many years people talked about it and he listened, but didn't seem to feel it was appropriate. I really have to say, and I think Mary would endorse this because we were both involved in it, that the great impetus for a European school came mainly through the focus of the Saanen Gatherings.

MZ: Yes, it was actually in 1966 that he started talking about a European school, to my knowledge. In the subsequent year, in 1967, when a group of people who were very eager about a Krishnamurti school wanted to discuss it, he held a meeting at Chalet Tannegg in Gstaad, and about fifty people came. He didn't talk very much, he listened to what they had in mind. A lot of them were quite effusive and rather sentimental—'Oh, we must have a Krishnamurti school'—and he didn't comment. But about a week later he called in about a dozen people, whom he seemed to think were really serious. I don't know why I was included because I had had nothing to do with schools at all, but I fortunately went, and he said to us, 'Are you serious? Do you know what it takes to do a school?' Out of that, after considerable discussion, came the fact that he wanted it to be an international school, preferably bilingual in French and English. And where to have it? Well, the candidate countries were Switzerland, England, Holland and France. And so he appointed one person or a small group from each country to go and explore the local situations, to find out what the circumstances of a school would be, the legalities and so forth, and report the following year.

So the following year, four reports came back. At that point in France de Gaulle was still in power, and one didn't know what would happen if he died, when conditions might change and make it difficult for the kind of education Krishnaji had in mind. So France was out. In Holland, the laws then were, maybe still are, that a proportion of the courses had to be taught in Dutch, and that made the language problem complicated. He already knew that he would like Dorothy and Montague Simmons to run the school. Switzerland, by the way, had too many private schools and it was too expensive and we had no money. So by elimination it became England.

MC: Yes. When the decision was finally made, it was with complete agreement among the people from these other countries who had been exploring conditions. In England there were several of us looking; Dorothy and Montague, David and Saral Bohm and myself were exploring conditions here. One of the things that also seemed to affect Krishnaji quite deeply—and interestingly enough it came up this morning on that bit of the tape that we heard when he was talking about education and caring for our children—England, or Britain I should say, was one of the few European major states at that time which did not have military conscription. I was shocked this morning to hear that some countries in Europe still have it. That certainly seemed to predispose Krishnaji towards a school in England. And of course, the language; Krishnaji gave his talks in English and that obviously was a big factor.

When we were in Switzerland, and there was this enormous focus of interest, it was a very international gathering. In many ways it was a very young gathering, although people of all ages were there, and he was speaking to his new, if I may put it this way, post-war and also post-Theosophist audience. There were still people who had heard him speak at Ommen in Holland but there were many, many people who had come to it fresh without any of the Theosophical background. I think he felt the time was right for a school. There was something in the air in the mid-1960s.

Stephen Smith: It was the end of the '60s, wasn't it?

MC: Well, it was in the mid-'60s that he seemed to begin to feel we could move towards a school. And, of course, Dorothy Simmons came on the scene around '66, '67, I think.

MZ: She was one of the group that he asked to come back after this big meeting of fifty people. Dorothy was in that, and he very quickly decided that she should be the Principal of the School.

MC: And David Bohm was also very much in evidence in all this. He talked a great deal with Dorothy and Montague, of course, with Krishnaji and one or two people who were interested in possibly becoming staff at the School. I think Dorothy and Montague's involvement considerably helped Krishnaji feel this was the time to do it. It might be interesting just to talk a bit about Dorothy and Montague's rather interesting educational contribution before they came to Brockwood. Dorothy Simmons, the first Principal of Brockwood, was not an academic. She was a sculptor, and she had this wonderful rapport with all people, but particularly with young people.

Montague had been a headmaster; he had also been an Inspector of schools, and his work had brought him into contact with intelligent delinquent boys who were at certain special schools in Britain. Montague made the point that these boys were sent to these corrective schools because they were delinquent, but they came out of them rather worse than when they went in, with their delinquency consolidated. He felt these schools were not really coping with them, and apparently the Home Office said: you feel this, so you start a school for delinquent boys with high IQs and see what you can do. And he and Dorothy actually ran such a school with, apparently, remarkable and very positive results. So that was Dorothy's background; she wasn't a teacher but she had been used to working with young people, and often young people with considerable problems. So the work of starting the School began. Once Krishnaji was sure we were going ahead, he seemed almost impatient to start.

MZ: Yes, he was pushing to find a place to start the school. And again we, as usual, had no money at all. A donor and admirer of Krishnaji wanted to give him a home to retire to in the south of France, a French farmhouse. But, in fact, he never really intended to retire. And so when the school idea was growing he asked this person, 'Would it be possible to spend what it would cost to get the farmhouse on a school?' The donor said, 'Whatever you want, of course.' So that meant we had enough, not a lot in terms of today, but what turned out to be almost exactly the cost of this place. Other houses were looked at, and Krishnaji was pushing, pushing to get a place.

MC: Well, first we looked at a rather lovely place in Buckinghamshire which was charming, beautiful, but turned out to have all sorts of structural faults. And then we looked at the former home of the film-star, Dirk Bogarde, a place called Nor, which was also charming but hardly big enough or suitable for a school. But Dorothy, of course, was enthusiastic and I said to her, 'Well, where would you and Montague actually live, because it's not very large?' 'Oh', she said, 'we'll live in the garage'! But it would not have worked out. Krishnaji was then away, and this is when he sent that rather famous telegram, which said, 'Buy it and plant a thousand daffodils'. Well, we didn't actually buy Nor, but eventually we got *this* place where there were already perhaps a thousand daffodils, but we probably planted another thousand.

MZ: He wanted, I think, also a place either with a little house nearby or something suitable for him to live in. And we are now sitting in his end of the house [the West wing]. That's one reason Brockwood was liked so much: Krishnaji could have his own quarters, and yet we'd all be in one place.

MC: I think another interesting thing was the way the School started. Once the decision had been made that we were going to have a school and it was a question of finding the premises, Krishnaji got so enthusiastic that he was partly instrumental in getting at least two students, one from India, one from America, two young boys, who came here. So Dorothy was actually carting these students around the country with her, looking for the premises. There used to be a well-known play called something like "So many Characters in Search of an Author". I thought this was rather funny, two students in search of their school! Anyway, Brockwood Park School actually opened in 1969.

MZ: Yes. It opened with a few more students, but not many, in September '69. I've looked it up, so I can tell you. In December 1968 we signed the contract, and we took possession of the place in January '69, when Dorothy, Montague and Doris Pratt moved in.

MC: Doris was Secretary of the old Krishnamurti Writings before me, and then she came here as Dorothy's secretary.

MZ: They had to start repainting and refurbishing everything. Huge work went on here, done mostly by just those of us involved, not outside people.

MC: Dorothy had a wonderful capacity for organizing people into what she called work parties. And she used to have these weekends when helpers would come. Compared with now the place was, well I won't say dilapidated, but it needed a great deal of attention, and she had them all beavering here, working and digging and painting and doing all sorts of jobs. It really was great, the effort and the co-operation that went into it. It was always a beautiful place, there was no question about that, but a lot had to be, and was, done.

Questioner: I remember that, because I was one of the early beavers in 1969.

MC: Well you'll remember how very hard everyone worked. I think Dorothy seemed to have some fund of people too, whom she knew from previous incarnations, or previous parts of her existence, who had been Gurdjieffians; I believe the people who are interested in Gurdjieff are usually terribly hard workers!

Krishnaji, of course, was very involved from the very beginning. Obviously he couldn't be here all the time because he spent much of every year in India and in America, and at that time he was still giving talks in the capital cities of Europe—Paris, Amsterdam, Rome, London. But he did spend several months of every year at Brockwood, and it was then his home. And I think it's true to say he was involved in relationship here with the staff and the students in a way which was perhaps different from any other school that he was associated with, partly because of the older age-range of the students, and partly because he was talking all the time to the students and to the staff. I feel he was absolutely at the heart of it, and the way it developed. Also, when he wasn't here, he started to write the *Letters to the Schools,* which were marvellous. These were shared with all the schools, so it was a way of linking them, and it was also a way of keeping a close contact with Krishnaji when he wasn't here. If any of you don't know about these *Letters to the Schools,* they are still available in two volumes, modest sized little books but with marvellous things that one can read and re-read.

MZ: He dictated these, sometimes one or two a day. And then he would hold them and say, 'Now send them out on the 1st and the 15th of the month', or sometimes it was monthly, so they would reach all the schools at the same time. This is just to give you an indication. Although he wanted other schools to listen to what he was teaching, he felt responsible for only the schools which he could visit, and which therefore could bear his name. He didn't want other schools to use his name because he said he couldn't be responsible for what they did. If he couldn't spend time in them he couldn't be responsible. And obviously his time was full. So the *Letters* were a way of spreading to other schools what he was saying; he wanted them published, so we, of course, did publish them, for anyone who was interested.

MC: I think another thing, which Mary and I were reminding ourselves of, was that from the very early days Krishnaji really saw Brockwood as "more than a school". Obviously, his concern was to establish here an atmosphere in which young minds could flower, be open. Also, of course, that there should be this quality of life here for everybody associated with the School, for the teachers and anyone else who was working here, and the people who were visiting and coming to the place. I think he felt that the people who were seriously interested in the teachings who would come to Brockwood, not necessarily as staff or students, would also have some input in this place. And that it would work both ways: the School would have an effect on them, they would have an effect on the School. He talked about this a great deal over the years.

At a certain point he really began to feel we should have an adult centre here, and the cloisters was built, originally as an adult centre. The cloister concept was very interesting with individual rooms, but a communal sitting room and the feeling of the cloister. Unfortunately, in a way, the School grew so rapidly that it began to take over the cloister accommodation so that it never quite fulfilled its role as an adult centre, although there was always some visitor accommodation. It is very interesting that some years after this, Krishnaji came up again very strongly and deeply with the idea, and felt the real imperative for an adult centre. And that, of course, was when the Krishnamurti Centre that you now know was envisaged and, soon after he died, was built.

SS: How was the name "cloisters" come upon, because it seems incongruous in a sense?

MZ: The shape of it, I think.

SS: Just the shape?

MC: The architect designed it that way. First of all there was another design which was rather more conventional and I don't think Krishnaji ever really liked that design. I remember we were talking about this; we hadn't any money, the usual situation, so how could we build an adult centre? And several trustees talked about it, and after a great deal of cogitation, decided that we couldn't possibly build as we hadn't any money, but that we might have caravans or, you know, "Portacabins", and so have some sort of adult centre. And Krishnaji sat there very quietly while all this was going on and the decision was actually made that we couldn't possibly build. A couple of people who were particularly worried about the finances left the room and Krishnaji turned to Dorothy Simmons and said, 'Now, Mrs D, what sort of building shall we have?' We somehow had moved from a building which was rather ordinary, which we couldn't afford, to Portacabins, which we possibly could afford, to this completely new concept, which became the cloisters. I think it was just that, that the architect saw it that way and it seemed, in a way, to fit the need. Do you feel it's incongruous?

SS: Well, the name is strange.

Ray McCoy: It has something in common with mediaeval cloisters. You know, the covered walkway around, and it's sort of closed off from everything.

MC: Well Krishnaji did actually use that name, and he also used to talk of an 'ashrama' sometimes, although I know this has become rather a "dirty" word.

MZ: He spoke of an ashram but he thought it was too religious.

MC: So he dropped that.

MZ: The thing that was always very strong about this place, and the School, was atmosphere. Krishnaji felt that one of the essentials in a school was the atmosphere, which is brought about among all the people living there—the staff, teachers, the students. And I remember him saying, and

103

rather terrorizing the staff by doing so, 'Students who come here for the first time must feel the atmosphere, feel there is something different when they cross the cattle grid'. Now the cattle grid is right over by the end of those trees. And they should be seized by this extraordinary atmosphere. And everybody thought, 'God, how can we bring that about?' But the answer is, in a way, in his teachings, which say, and I think this is borne out, that there is an atmosphere when people together are seriously concerned with right relationship with each other, regardless of whatever job they are doing. They do create something—can we call it atmosphere?—which is very powerful and very real and very important. And I think this has been the basis for Brockwood and the other schools founded by Krishnaji. They have tried also to bring about a special relationship among all the people involved; in particular the staff are responsible to bring this about as much as possible with the students. There are wonderful quotations here. For instance, Krishnaji said, 'It is very important that the child feels secure from the very first day. The first impression must give this. This allows the natural curiosity of the child to bring about a state of inquiring, and only then can there be learning.' But it was all from this almost subliminal sense that the child would have. And it was interesting to me this morning, when some of you talked to the students, that several of them when asked, 'What did you feel when you came here?', said immediately, 'I'm at home'. It was, to me, very moving to hear that from nineteen-year-olds.

MC: Arising from what Mary has just said, the question has been asked over the years, why a school? Why not a community or a group? Because obviously people come here to work because they are attracted by the teachings, that is what their starting point is. Why a school? But I think Krishnaji has answered this in his books and talks. I remember we were having a meeting, talking about Brockwood and wondering if we should think differently. Should we think, perhaps, of not having a school? Should we think of having Brockwood only as an adult centre, and so on. Then Stephen Smith said—if I can paraphrase you, Stephen—'Well, you know there are lots of things we could do to live according to the teachings, but there is something about a school which has a sense of service'. I think the school at Brockwood has this service in the deep sense of the word that Krishnaji meant. To me this is the wonderful thing about Brockwood. With all the vicissitudes and all the difficulties, I feel that this has always been there.

MZ: To underline what you just said with a quote that I like: 'The teacher who finds what existence means, who is really teaching, has a primary place in civilisation'. A tremendous statement.

For years I kept notes of things that Krishnaji would say, not in public talks but in conversations. And the night before last I was rustling through these and I came upon something that I really would like to read to you. This was dated July 30th 1975, which means it would have been in Switzerland. He was talking about responsibility and he said:

Responsibility is not to the students but to "the other",

[MZ: "the other" is in quotes, and I think most of you will know what he meant by that.]

and that responsibility will translate itself into daily life. There is a need at Brockwood to move to a dimension where a flame of energy is always abundant. I am responsible to that, I am totally committed to that, not to tradition. Traditional energy is a total wastage of energy but in "the other" there is more and more and more. So we need leisure, space to find out how to convey that in education. How is a student to have that dimension, that flame? How do we bring this about? That is education, not by authority, compulsion, imitation, reward and punishment. I abandon all those ways. I want the child to have no problems. Is there some catalyst that will shatter all his conditioning and when he comes to Brockwood the thing is broken? In one week to uncondition the student. How? By bringing about an atmosphere, a seriousness, real affection in the air, disturbing but interesting, a sense of stability, abiding reverence in that immutable truth, unchangeable reality.

One sees what he really wanted in education. I find such an eloquence in that.

MC: I think it's interesting how the age group evolved at Brockwood. Obviously a school can be of small children; it can be a middle school, junior school, secondary school and so on. Somehow it seemed quickly to fall into place that Brockwood would be a school for older students. This was something different from what Krishnaji had done before. It was a new approach. Krishnaji seemed very much to feel this was something we could do here. Over the years there has been a lot of discussion about extending the age group range to include younger children. We actually extended it upwards. We have students here who are, of course, much older than students in many schools.

There was one remarkable day when Krishnaji came back from India. The pattern often was that he would talk in India, come back to Brockwood for a few days, then go on to America before coming back again to Brockwood and to Saanen later in the year. I know that Dorothy Simmons would often rather dread his return from India. She would say, 'Every time Krishnaji comes back from India, he comes full of all these new feelings and passion'. She always felt that everything was going to be turned upside down from top to tail, which it often was. Some of the greatest challenges he seemed to present us with were when he came back from India. And on one occasion he came back and the trustees and some staff members spent a whole, and a really rather trying day talking about Brock-wood. Krishnamurti seemed most passionate that we should extend the age range *downwards*. Not only that, but we should open our doors to babies! And of course this was open to interesting interpretation among some of the staff! But suddenly, I don't know how it happened, the whole feeling changed, and by the end of the day Krishnaji and everyone was saying, 'Well, we should really have students who are *older* than those we have already'. You know, we went through this extraordinary process, and actually then agreed that we were going to have students a little bit older, starting around 14 or 15, and not have the 12- or 13-year-olds. Of course this was the extraordinary thing about Krishnaji, this openness; it was also very chal-lenging to be with. Mary, I'm sure you have some thoughts on that in the Ojai school.

MZ: Yes. The Ojai school, which is called the Oak Grove School, which was talked about in the Krishnamurti Foun-dation of America in the mid-'70s, finally began in 1977. Krishnaji had said about the school, 'Let us try with younger students up to the age of entry to Brockwood. Let's see if we can get younger children, because then they would be less conditioned'. So the decision was made to start with kindergarten. Of course, at that point a residential school was not considered because the children were too young. But in an extraordinary way families who heard about Krishnamurti's teachings, picked up their lives, gave up their jobs, sometimes their houses, and moved to Ojai to put their children in a Krishnamurti school. We started out with just a handful, and it now is much bigger, about 125 students at the moment. When those children had to decide what to do when they reached high school age, there was a tremendous push among the parents. They didn't want to send their children, who had been at Oak Grove, out of a Krishnamurti school and education to go to the local high school. So there was a campaign, and finally Krishnaji and the trustees agreed that we would have a high school. It didn't have to be residential, but we *do* have residential places. We can take about 40 students. So it now covers kindergarten right up through high school. And that all started in 1977.

As mentioned earlier, after leaving India, Krishnaji would come here briefly and then go on to Ojai with similar challenges; only at Oak Grove School he stressed the importance of parental participation. With Brockwood, of course, the parents are so all over the world, in different countries, but in Ojai the parents largely live in the Valley, so they play a tremendous part in the school, and he would talk to them. I remember one winter in Ojai when he held forty different discussions, two or three hour discussions, with parents and staff, and worked very, very hard. So the difference in the Ojai school is that it is only partly residential, and it does take a lot of children, and the parents are extremely involved. It is quite different, but they are trying to do exactly what Brockwood is trying to do in the sense of communicating at all levels what Krishnaji wanted and had in mind.

MC: Perhaps I should say here too that with Krishnaji nothing was ever set in concrete, and this place has evolved during his time, and of course since. There has been an initiative recently, of which some of you may be aware. Some of the staff who live and work here have started a pre-school group for their own very young children, and it is in a separate building down the road. They are also opening this a little bit to the children from the village here. This is a fresh development, and some of us hope it might eventually become a junior school, but we have to see how that will go.

Krishnamurti never really made rules at Brockwood, and rules are still kept to the minimum. However, he did have a profound effect on the whole ethos. Mary mentioned earlier that many students who come here get the feeling that this is home. Krishnaji often talked with the staff too about it being their home, but equally he would say that it should be possible for them to be able to walk away without dependence on or attachment to it, which was extremely interesting. I do not live here, but I can see that it must be difficult sometimes for people who have lived and worked here to walk away. That's something that people who live here would be able to talk about.

His involvement with the School was tremendously deep. We have, of course, a lot of his dialogues with staff and students on tapes, some of them in books. As well as *Letters to the Schools*, there is a book called *The Beginnings of Learning*, which many of you will know. Much of that comprises Krishnaji's discussions with students from various Krishnamurti schools, and with parents and teachers. I find his dialogues with the schools truly remarkable. At one level these were so down to earth, dealing with what we call the nitty-gritty of running a school, but in other ways they would touch on something, which seemed limitless. One is struck by the fact that his definitions of things like "discipline", "order", "concentration" or "attention" always had extraordinary freshness and aptness.

I wonder if I could share one of them with you? This is from *The Beginnings of Learning*. I'm not going to read the whole dialogue, obviously, but it has been a discussion about concentration and attention, and this is how he brings it to an end. Having been talking very specifically about all this, he says:

Concentration is a form of resistance, it's a form of exclusion, a shutting out, a retreat, but attention is something quite different. In concentration there is a centre from which the action of observation takes place. Where there is a centre, the radius of its observation is very limited. Where there is no centre observation is vast, clear. This is attention.

Now someone says, 'I'm afraid we don't understand this at all, sir'. Krishnamurti goes on—this discussion took place in India:

Look out at those hills, see the light on them, see those trees, hear the bullock carts going by, see the yellow leaves, the dry riverbed and that crow sitting on the branch. Look at all of this. If you look from a centre with its prejudice, with its fear, with its like and dislike, then you don't see the vast expanse of this earth. Then your eyes are clouded, then you become myopic and your eyesight becomes twisted. Can you look at all this, the beauty of the valley, the sky, without a centre? Then that is attention. Then listen with attention and without the centre to another's criticism, insult, anger, prejudice. Because there is no centre in that attention there is no possibility of being hurt. But when there is a centre

110

there is inevitable hurt. Then life becomes one scream of fear.

I thought you would find it interesting to see just how he talked with the staff and students about these things, which are so near to home and yet take in so much.

MZ: Well, I have also a quotation from Krishnaji, something I found. This not in a book but in my notes, but I'd like to read it because it struck me so tremendously. And again, it's in conversation. He said:

There are two fields, goodness and hate. There is also another field, which goes beyond the two. Man spends most of his capacity in hate and not in goodness. There is an energy which does not belong to either. Both these belong to man. War creates an atmosphere, so does goodness. Both are within man's capacity. To move within these is still tradition. There is another area which, if we can touch it, gives an energy which doesn't belong to either. I believe we can touch it, and when we do, that will transform what we are doing. If we can open the door to it, it will operate. There is an energy which is not manmade. You can't get to it by manmade ways, by vows, chastity, poverty. But man has asked if there is an area where manmade things do not exist. Can we as a group discern that, recognizing that what is manmade is incomplete? Is there something that is totally complete and can my mind capture it, an area where miracles happen, where something new exists, a state from which all life flows, the beginning of everything? Can we come to that? Otherwise we are treading in this field, tradition. It is my responsibility to come to that. I will not have my roots in these. I may have no roots and therefore be open to the width of the heavens.

MC: I think the intensity of the dialogues he had with the staff, the students and everyone involved in the schools was remarkable and sustained over a long period. We know how hard he worked for the schools. When Dorothy was Principal, he spent a great deal of time talking with her, walking with her, going into every aspect of the School, of the students and their needs and so on. When Dorothy became ill and a group was formed of four and then five, I know that he gave a great deal of energy to being with them, and then, when Scott was the Principal, with Scott. He did this also with "the fourteen", a group of people who had then been here for some time. Towards the end of Krishnaji's life, he regarded them as a kind of nucleus group. I think he felt that here we had a group of people who would create what we talked about earlier, this atmosphere, this *right* atmosphere, and this would then go on from that nucleus group to the new staff, and so on, and extend. There are several people in this room, I think, who were part of that group who could talk about it better than I can.

MZ: Krishnaji was very concerned about what would happen to all this when he was gone. He often used to say to us in meetings, 'I'm gone, I'm dead, what are you going to do now?' He was in a way preparing us for the responsibility, which was on him. People worked extraordinarily hard, but still he did carry the schools, or at least the one here at Brockwood. I can't speak for India, but he had tremendous influence there. He wanted people to come to a realization of the things that he talked about, so that it would be a living thing in them. He said, 'Books don't matter, it must be a living thing'; and he was trying to bring that about in all of us, staff, students, teachers, audiences, everybody who came anywhere near his teachings. From this particularly intensive contact with him one felt that, when he was gone, there would be a continuity that wouldn't flag or wouldn't go downhill, as it were. It was to me almost a sacred responsibility that he was putting to us.

Do you want to ask questions? I think that is enough of us.

MC: I wonder whether I could just mention one other aspect of his deep and consistent involvement with the work of the schools. He talked a great deal also with the trustees of the School here and also with some of the staff, and I remember one memorable occasion when we were going to write something about Brockwood for the Bulletin. This was probably when it had been in existence for ten years or so and we wanted to give a picture through the Bulletin of what was going on. It is actually very difficult to write about what is really happening in a place like Brockwood, especially when one wants to do it with absolute honesty. The discussion didn't take off very creatively, and then Krishnamurti said to every person in the room, 'What are we doing at Brockwood?' He made everyone individually answer this question, which was really very difficult, because first of all people would say, "We are trying to ...", and of course he wouldn't allow the word "trying", or "we think". 'What are we *actually* doing at Brockwood?', was his question. And, whatever anyone said he didn't seem to feel that the answers were adequate. Indeed, sometimes he would sort of wince and turn away, as if some terrible thing had been said. And one really hoped by the time he came to oneself that the floor would open up before one had to answer the question, but it wasn't so! At the end, when we had all had our say, Krishnamurti just sat there very, very quietly and apparently not offering any help at all, but with that tremendous inward look that he had when his eyelids would come down and you felt you were in the presence of something remarkable, some sort of power-house of inner energy, and you hardly dared to speak. However, I did take courage and say, 'Krishnaji, can we ask you this question, what are we doing at Brockwood?' This seemed the obvious thing to do, to ask him. And he said, 'Oh, it's quite simple. We are making new human beings'. Well, it *may* be simple, but so much was involved in this. Then after some pause for reflection I said to him, 'Can we put this in the Bulletin?' Because, you know, we were writing this article for the Bulletin. And he said, 'Yes, of course'. Anyway, two days later I had a telephone call from him and he said, 'I think perhaps we should not put that in'. I don't know exactly what it did mean, but in his heart that was what we were doing: making new human beings at Brockwood Park—a tremendous challenge to everybody who is here, who is involved with that.

Q: Has he ever talked about new schools after his death, starting new schools without his help?

MC: He did talk about this because this question frequently came up. As Mary said, he was wondering and talking about what would happen after he died.

MZ: He wanted new schools, obviously, but felt that he could only be responsible for schools that bore his name if he personally visited them, and was concerned with them. He felt that otherwise he couldn't be responsible, but that didn't mean there shouldn't be schools. And I believe in India a couple of new schools have started.

Kabir: The point is that when Krishnaji was alive he was very concerned with having schools and having people who

114

were deeply responsible for bringing about a new quality in education. And in fact the Krishnamurti Foundation in India have started new schools in Poona. It's part of the Krishnamurti Foundation. And in some sense it seems to me that if we don't do it, if we don't do it in the right way and if we don't do it taking the full responsibility, we are merely transferring the responsibility to him and saying that as long as he was alive we could do something and now we can't do anything more. It was not just his responsibility for the teachings but in some sense we are all responsible.

MC: This point did come up, Kabir. And I think the point you make is a very profound one. We can't leave the responsibility with Krishnamurti only, obviously. In Saanen once, when the International Committees were discussing this very question of starting new schools, he made the point again that he felt it was better not to associate his name with schools that he hadn't actually worked in or been in some way responsible for. But we did discuss the question of new schools. New schools would start inevitably, and one would want schools to be inspired by Krishnamurti. And he went so far then as to say, 'Well, this is up to the Foundations'. Also, of course, existing Krishnamurti schools will probably open out and expand. If it is felt that a new school that begins somewhere is sympathetic with the whole ethos of the Krishnamurti schools, then that school could perhaps be brought into this network, although not necessarily be an official school of the Foundation. This expression was used, "to become part of this network", which I think is a very good way of looking at it.

MZ: There's a slight offshoot of this question. The American Foundation early on started so-called Krishnamurti

Centres around the country where people would show tapes, hold meetings and provide books and so forth. And they were called Krishnamurti Centres. Well, we came to realize that, in effect, we could never visit them because America was too big and we didn't have people to do it, we had to trust people. But some of the Centres were functioning inappropriately, and they were using Krishnamurti's name, while whoever was running things would become the local guru and hold forth. And so we withdrew the use of the Krishnamurti Foundation's name. In other words, people in their own houses can show tapes—we can't prevent it—but they can't be listed in the Krishnamurti Foundation of America Bulletin as Krishnamurti Centres as before. This doesn't mean that lots of people aren't indeed showing tapes and providing a very useful service, but the responsibility for using Krishnamurti's name was felt strongly, and we must protect that.

Now, of course, with the Internet, things are burgeoning all over the place. Anybody can start anything they want, including a Krishnamurti page. It is something that has to be treated with responsibility and sensitivity because, above all, Krishnaji used to say, 'Don't let people interpret'. And of course there is often the temptation to interpret, to explain what Krishnamurti really meant, to someone, and that was what was happening in some of these Centres. People were saying, 'Well, I'll explain it to you'. That is precisely what he asked all of us who had anything to do with his work *not* to let happen, and certainly not to do it ourselves. You can't police people but at least you can try to keep it clear. Nobody has a right to interpret. He said very clearly, 'Nobody has ever spoken for me, nobody speaks for me today, and nobody speaks for me in the future with regard to the teachings'. He had that published, because someone was already claiming to succeed him when he died. So this is a question to be treated with great sensitivity and respect.

MC: We are a very small group of people really, and the same applies in all the different countries. But there *will* be schools, and one knows that there will be the inspiration of Krishnaji as an educator.

MZ: Any questions?

MC: Or comments? People who work here in the School might like to add something to what we've said.

Q: I'd like to hear the two of you carry on talking for days! Is there any possibility, Mary, that you might consider having some of these wonderful quotations published?

MZ: Well, I am supposed to—*supposed* underlined. Krishnaji asked me on several occasions, and Mary Lutyens regrettably mentioned it in her book that he had asked me, to write "what it is like to be with that man", as he put it. In the beginning, I felt it impossible to express adequately what this man was like, but eventually I came to feel that anything in history, whether an event, a person, a discovery or anything else is conveyed through the testimony of people who were witnesses. That seems to be the way life works. So I feel there is a responsibility for those who have known Krishnaji to leave some record. Those pieces become what I think of as a mosaic. As I happened to have the extraordinary privilege to be somewhat involved in the last twenty years of his life, and as he asked me to write about it, I am doing so using the notes I kept for many years. But whatever results, there will always be for me the sense that beyond any words lies something vast, untouchable and unknowable that is the reality of Krishnamurti's life.

MC: It's very important. I am writing something too, which is a sort of history of working with him over many years. I have written several books on different subjects—but writing about this is very, very different and very, very challenging, because it would be so easy to embroider, to add to the myths. One doesn't want to do that. One is not concerned with myth-making when one is writing about Krishnamurti or his work. One has to watch scrupulously how one puts things, what one says. Like Mary, I have written certain things down over the years, but of course one is often relying on memory, and to some extent it is personal interpretation of situations. If you took, for instance, any situation in which Krishnamurti is talking with six people, if they all went away and wrote it up afterwards it would be most interesting to see how they did so. And I think we would find that there might be six different versions. You know, the gospel according to Matthew, Mark, Luke and John, or whatever it is, the gospel according to Mary, Mary, Stephen, Claudia, Dominique, or whatever! And one does have to be so careful, because with Krishnamurti one is in the presence of something quite indefinable, and also, in a way quite, extremely vivid. It would be so easy to put the emphasis on the wrong words or even the wrong inflections—you know what it is like when you are talking with someone—it's the way he would speak, or the way he would stress things. So it is not easy. That's why this kind of memoir, or writing or history is very slow. But I think it has to be done, because the more people who do it, the more multifaceted the reporting is.

MZ: That way the mosaic has more pieces and there is more likelihood of something emerging that may make a clearer picture of this man who seems so impossible to explain.

118

MC: But the teachings are there and one then trusts to the intelligence of whoever reads it all to make their own response.

MZ: I don't know if I can finish it and if it ever will be published, but finished or unfinished, I would leave it in the archives so it would be a source for future people who are doing research. Because to me it's reporting; it's a memoir, if you like, but I look at it as a reporter because already a great deal of untruth has been said about Krishnamurti and so I feel that there must be a true record. And to the best of my knowledge, that's what I am writing.

MC: I think you were going to say something.

Q: You said Krishnamurti spoke of making new human beings, but still in a school somewhere else he mentioned that one should function in the chronological world. What happens with certificates, licenses, qualifications? I believe Krishnaji himself never obtained such things, diplomas or degrees. But the students who come here, how much effort is spent in that area? Or is the assumption that a new human being would be able to tackle also this, certificates, examination, the diploma? When you get out of Brockwood Park School you may be over and above these papers. Does the School consider that these papers are essential and try to provide the students with them?

MC: Well, this is a big question. Are you talking about the whole period, or now?

MZ: We don't give diplomas, but who from the School would know? Ray, you would know.

Ray McCoy: It's a question that's often asked: how do we deal with academics here? You'll see, when you read *Letters to the Schools* that Krishnamurti stressed that if we are

119

to do academics then, like everything else, they must be done excellently. That's fine for him to say. So all we have to do is to find teachers who can teach their subjects excellently and who want to be here and who also have some interest in Krishnamurti. Well, all of our teachers are here out of an interest in Krishnamurti; and all the students who want to study academics and to do exams are encouraged to do so. The emphasis is on something else though. The emphasis is on learning to be a whole human being. But of course being a whole human being also includes, can include, academics. However, you don't need academics to live a good life, so all of these things are put before the students and it's up to them. Of course, most of the pressure for them to do academics comes from their parents. So we do teach as many of the academic subjects here as we can, and students do take exams. And many, many students go on to university and do extremely well.

Q: Do you mean to say that you teach and give grades? Say on a subject like biology or physics, how do you go about it?

RMc: We don't give grades, but we give reports to the parents twice a year on what the student has been doing in the classes, and how they are doing also as human beings.

Q: Work on the student himself to assess how his progress is.

RMc: Always, yes. This is very important.

Q: I don't think you have to rely completely on the student. With small numbers you have a very close contact with the student: what he knows, what he doesn't know, what his difficulties are, where one should strengthen something. So one can do all that assessment for oneself without necessarily having to give a test to find out. I think with a small number of students that is possible. Day to day the teachers know where the student is.

Q: May I say something? My daughter who went to Oak Grove school, and then came here before she graduated, needed transcripts in order to get into University. She had been accepted at Berkeley, but they put a hold on her registration because they didn't have the right kind of transcripts. And Colin Foster very kindly translated her reports into grades, and put it in the form they wanted to see. It was honest but in a different form. They accepted her at Berkeley and accepted the Brockwood grades as a transcript. We didn't know if it would translate back to America, but it did.

Q: I think they are doing international exams at Brockwood now.

Q: Yes, we have so many students, mainly from other European countries that recognize the baccalaureate and not necessarily the British A level.

MZ: There was a time when some of the eastern United States colleges would accept students on Brockwood's word. Scott used to visit most of them, and our students who went there did so well that it became accepted that, if Brockwood said a student was at a certain level academically, they accepted it.

SS: I think the point there is that the students are very self-motivated. They need to be self-motivated when they are here, and therefore when they go to university, the university will see a self-motivated student who will be able to work on his or her own. That's the advantage of a free-style education; the students are able to work off their own bat, with a minimum of guidance and instruction.

Q: It must have made an enormous difference to the whole atmosphere of the School when Krishnamurti died, and yet there is still a very powerful atmosphere here. As you say, as soon as you step across the threshold it is there.

MZ: As soon as you come across the cattle-grid!

Q: Is there anything that one can do to make sure that this not only stays but continues to grow and expand, because it seems to me that this is the core of it?

MC: I think it depends upon every person who lives here that there is constant alertness to this from the new people, and the people who have been here some time. I remember that just after Krishnaji died I had come back from America, and I visited Brockwood. As I walked into this place, there was something tremendous here. Krishnaji had died, but it was as if everybody in the School (I'm talking about the staff, perhaps more than the students) had suddenly grown up. Perhaps, in a way, when Krishnaji was alive he was a father to us all, and to some extent I think we did depend on him to do certain things. As someone just said, we mustn't keep going backwards and always depending on him.

MZ: He was pushing us not to. Dependence was an anathema to him.

MC: When he had gone, when I walked in the door, I felt as if this place was humming with something. And I think it is. Every person has to keep that flame alive. I don't think there is any more that one can do. But it's wonderful that you feel it is still here. And it's in the Krishnamurti Centre, which, of course, hadn't been built then. Krishnaji was very much a part of it, planning it and talking about it, but it was actually built after he died.

MZ: He talked about the feeling of security being a primary need in children: 'Security is not dependency'. He talked a great deal about this, especially toward the end of his life, and whether we were dependent on him. Dependency overwhelms the human psyche.

MC: I think it is interesting that a lot of people who come to the Centre now, and the students who come to the School, have never actually heard Krishnamurti speak. Of course, you could say that there might still be dependency, because you could be dependent upon somebody from reading a book or from watching a tape. I think it is very encouraging that it is by no means only people who heard him speak, who knew him, who come to the School and the Centre, as there could possibly be the danger of looking back and trying to re-create something.

There is always this awful feeling of responsibility working in this. I feel that we are not doing enough. We all know that we have to try to make this much more widely known, and to increase the awareness of what is going on in our schools and in the work generally. And it is hard to do it.

MZ: There is no such thing as enough! I have been asked by people if Krishnamurti was ever satisfied. He wanted it to be better, more. The idea of being satisfied wouldn't occur to him.

Q: When he asked what you are doing in this School, you explained so well the feeling of people not knowing exactly what words to use. It is a difficulty everybody experiences. At one meeting at Ojai I remember one of the teachers said, 'What do you sense there?' He said, 'Why do you ask me?' And the teacher said, 'Because of your integrity'. So that's why we do get tongue-tied. It's a difficulty for anybody.

MC: There was such an intensity, such a passion with Krishnaji on certain occasions that it was very hard to be with that. And I think to the people who worked here, who were involved constantly with this, it must have been tremendously inspiring, but also a gigantic challenge. There was no resting place, it seems to me. I think of the Schools as an energy source for the whole of the work, because I feel that from the schools so much has happened, does happen and will happen. We are already getting some people who were students coming back as teachers, or helping with the work of the Foundation. There is one person in this room who has been a student here, a teacher and is now a trustee of one of the Foundations. The schools are providing a tremendous sense of energy and, because we are involved with young people, there is a feeling that this is how the work might continue and be spread, which is very good.

We had meetings in Saanen for twenty-five years and there was something very right about the atmosphere there. The climate, of course, as in England, could never be relied upon to be dry and we had to have some covering, but we never had a building. We always had this rather beautiful tent or marquee in which Krishnamurti spoke. And there seemed to be something very appropriate about the fact that he would speak over a period of several weeks, thousand of people would come from all over the world and listen to him and, at the end of it, the tent came down and we all went away. There was a beauty about that, about not having a structure or a centre. It seemed right also for what Krishnamurti said. Yet, at the same time, there is a beauty about this place, or any of the places that he has worked in, and it seems that it is necessary always to have some organization, but to keep this simple.

Q: It seems one doesn't want it to be asphyxiating.

MZ: He made it very clear that the organizations were only to get the work done. Nobody involved in the organization had any status of any kind. You were just there to wash the dishes or teach algebra or clean the floor or be responsible for something, but it's entirely functional.

Q: What am I doing here? I'm washing the floor. Full stop!

Kabir: I've always felt somehow that for a teaching that says no authority, no method, no technique, no time, schools are a natural. I think it was a stroke of genius that he did not create a church but schools.

Q: There is another asphyxiating factor: finances, money. How do the schools stand?

Q: A great problem!

Q: You rely on donations—rely is not good enough.

MZ: What else is there?

Q: You live with the uncertainty. Brockwood or Krishna-murti says you live with the uncertainty.

MC: We are quite good at doing that, actually. The difficulty, of course, with the uncertainty, is that when you are undertaking to educate young people you do have the sense of responsibility to exist at least for the natural term of their educational needs. It is always a problem, this quest-ion of money. And one doesn't like to keep talking about it, yet one has to because the need is always there. Brockwood runs with a staff who take very small remuneration for the work they do. So you can see how dedicated people are who choose to come and work here, especially if it is over a long period. Also, of course, as far as the students are concerned, we do award a lot of scholarships, and we have to raise money for these. Another thing we should say here, which people aren't always aware of, is that Brockwood has made no compromises in its syllabus or its approach to education in order to obtain finance from certain other more conventional sources. We feel that it has been important to be true to the essence of the teachings as far as this is possible. At Brockwood we have always tried to put the teachings at the centre of things without really thinking too much about the financial ramifications. But the financial need is quite urgent at the moment and there are many areas in which we do need monetary assistance to maintain things here.

MZ: Krishnaji had a way, and said it many times to us. There was always something urgently needed and he would say very serenely, 'If what we are doing is right, the money will turn up'. It has, notably for instance in the Centre, which you have seen is a very beautiful, expensive building. We didn't have any money at all when that idea came about. And extraordinarily we were given a tremendously generous donation. The Centre was built. But when the money came, inflation came too, so we had the money to start it but not enough to finish it. And about six months into the building an elderly lady from another country, whom we had never met before, came to look at the School for, I think, a grandchild. She saw the building going up and said, 'What is that?' She was told what it was and said, 'What a good idea. Have you plenty of money?' Well the end of the story is that she gave us what was needed. But we actually started building the Centre without having enough money but remembering his saying that magic thing, and it magically happened again. This doesn't give us any undue sense of security today, but it has happened.

Brockwood Park, 16 August 1997